In the name of God, the Merciful, the Compassionate.

*Words of consecration used on a variety of occasions to call forth
divine benediction and sanctify everyday words and actions.*

Bismillah al-raḥmān al-raḥīm

DEVOTIONS

Wisdom from the Cradle of Civilization

DANIELLE AND OLIVIER FÖLLMI

With a contribution by Paolo Branca
Calligraphy by Ismet Bozbey

Rabbi Akiva ◆ Ibn 'Arabi ◆ 'Attar ◆ Saint Augustine ◆ Mursi Jamil 'Aziz ◆ Baal Shem Tov ◆ Ben Azzai ◆ Tahar Ben Jelloun ◆ Ben Zoma
Khaled Bentounès ◆ The Bible ◆ Philippe Yacine Demaison ◆ Rabbi Elisha ben Abuyah ◆ Yunus Emre ◆ Genesis ◆ al-Ghazali
Kahlil Gibran ◆ The Hadith ◆ Hafiz ◆ Rabbi Hanina ben Dosa ◆ Muhammad al-Harraq ◆ Hillel the Elder
Saint Isaac the Syrian ◆ Edmond Jabès ◆ Saint John ◆ Ahmad Shafiq Kamal ◆ Shaykh Abul-Hassan Kharaqani ◆ Omar Khayyám
The Qur'an ◆ Stanislas Jerzy Lec ◆ Saint Luke ◆ Amin Maalouf ◆ Naguib Mahfouz ◆ Saint Matthew ◆ Rabbi Meir
Rabbi Menachem Mendel of Kotsk ◆ Iraj Mirza ◆ Rabbi Moshe Leyb of Sassov ◆ Prophet Muhammad
Rabbi Nachman of Breslov ◆ George Nathan ◆ Marc-Alain Ouaknin ◆ Orhan Pamuk ◆ Saint Paul ◆ Ahmad Muhammad Rami
Rumi ◆ Frithjof Schuon ◆ Mahmud Shabistari ◆ Rabbi Shimon bar Yochai ◆ Rabbi Shmuel Shmelke of Nikolsburg
Rabbi Simcha Bunim of Pshiskha ◆ Faouzi Skali ◆ The Talmud ◆ Abu Hayyan al-Tawhidi ◆ Saint Thomas ◆ The Torah
Mahmud Bayram al-Tunisi ◆ Umm Kulthum ◆ Rabbi Yehuda ha-Nasi ◆ Rabbi Yitzchak Aisik the Hasid
Rabbi Yochanan ben Zakkai ◆ Rabbi Yose ben Halafta ◆ Muhammad Yunus ◆ Rabbi Zadok ha-Kohen of Lublin

ABRAMS, NEW YORK

JANUARY 1 TO MARCH 31
To Give Meaning

Pure heart

The great inner journey

To love through God

Perceive, listen, give meaning

Rely on the physical world

Sanctify the senses

The Soul is a source

Inebriation of love

Choose with wisdom

Mirages and illusions

Detachment

The joy of being alive

Know how to receive

APRIL 1 TO JUNE 30
To Give of Yourself

Like a mother gives life

The friend, the companion

The meeting of souls

The sharing of friendship

What you love, I love too

Purity, sincerity, integrity

The language of the heart

Words of mercy

Forgetting yourself

Listen to the depths of your soul

Loyalty, simplicity

Between asceticism and mysticism

Patience and modesty

JULY 1 TO SEPTEMBER 30
Giving and Forgiving

The rules of the spirit
Knowing and Being
Be!
What is good in you
Love of humankind
Responsibility is intelligence
The value of the intention
Hopes for your brother
Mercy and magnanimity
Work of compassion
When forgiveness liberates
Goodness and charity
To withhold is to perish

OCTOBER 1 TO DECEMBER 31
May Peace Be with You

Whoever you are, come!
You just have to know yourself
No truth, no peace
One step against poverty
Part of the adventure
Brotherhood, solidarity
Inner peace
Liberty and grace
Love is the universal order
God is beautiful and loves beauty
To be reborn in Unity
Devotions
The mystery of mysteries

Foreword

And behold, the Lord passed by, and a great and strong wind tore the mountains and broke in pieces the rocks before the Lord, but the Lord was not in the wind. And after the wind an earthquake, but the Lord was not in the earthquake. And after the earthquake a fire, but the Lord was not in the fire. And after the fire the sound of a low whisper. And when Elijah heard it, he wrapped his face in his cloak and went out and stood at the entrance of the cave. (1 Kings 19:11–13)

This famous passage from the Bible reminds us that revelation of the absolute is often not accompanied by the extraordinary signs we might expect, given their mysterious and awesome origin.

By means of a journey in images and texts reflecting the great cultural and religious traditions of North Africa and the Middle East, this book leads us from the arid, superficial nature of our modern ways to the very sources of life. Paradoxically, the desert regions of the Middle East and North Africa are the principal protagonists of this return to the source. Yet it should not surprise us. Judaism, Christianity, and Islam share common roots in Abraham, the nomadic patriarch whose life jostles our certainties and provokes us to take to the road.

From start to finish, the proposed itinerary is rich in anticipation and a sense of the quest. The answer—which is different for everyone, yet unique to all of us—is given to those who know how to question themselves: This is

probably the key to the mystery that pulses in every stone, every breath, and every life in this authentic cradle of humanity. Those with access to this mystery are not the privileged few blessed with particular means and knowledge, but every human being who hears the call to become a child again and is thus capable of humility, curiosity, and surprise. In this context, each prophecy returns to what it should always be and remain: not rigorously formulated dogma, but an unhoped-for insight into the enigma of our origins as well as a sign of what awaits us in the beyond.

All beings conscious of this mystery—not just the religious-minded—will recognize themselves in this journey. Questions we had not yet expressed—and sometimes had not even been clearly aware of—arise on every page, casting the vestiges of a history as old as the world back onto the simplest, most familiar everyday experiences.

It is as if we had reached the peak of a mountain after a slow ascent. No matter how long the road traveled, eventually we could see new and unsuspected horizons open up before us. We would be moved by this gift and grateful for it. And we would immediately want to share it, so that we and those we love could have the privilege of seeing ourselves and our world in a completely new light.

Paolo Branca

PROFESSOR OF ARABIC LANGUAGE AND LITERATURE
AND ISLAMIC CULTURE
CATHOLIC UNIVERSITY OF THE SACRED HEART
MILAN, ITALY

In the vessel of time the world pursues its voyage, without harbor or shore, toward infinity. For it is here, my friend, in this very world, that passing time and eternity are joined.

Faouzi Skali
20TH–21ST CENTURY

In the Saharan region of Awbari, the last oasis of the Wadi al-Ajal, Libya.

God hides—so people search for Him.

Rabbi Nachman of Breslov
18TH–19TH CENTURY

The monastic compound built to house the monks on the heights of the isolated Coptic monastery of Saint Paul of Thebes (Deir Mar Boulos) in Egypt contains five churches.

For the breath of life is in the sunlight

and the hand of life is in the wind.

Kahlil Gibran

20TH CENTURY

In Ghat, on the edge of the Sahara Desert in Libya.

Be melting snow.

Wash yourself of yourself.

Rumi
13TH CENTURY

Dromedaries come to drink from the Guelta Archei in Chad in the southern Sahara.

If we become aware that each one of us is an aspect of the face of God—like the facet of a diamond—

then we can adore God in brotherhood and mutual love.

Khaled Bentounès

20TH–21ST CENTURY

Four-year-old Wamusabri in Ghadames, Libya, during the annual celebration where Berber and Tuareg families revive their traditions.

You lack a foot to travel?

Then journey into yourself—

That leads to transformation

of dust into pure gold.

Rumi
13TH CENTURY

A caravan crosses a perennial patch of snow in the High Altai mountains of Mongolia.
OVERLEAF: In Aswan, Egypt, merchandise is still transported on the Nile, but the feluccas are used mostly for tourism.

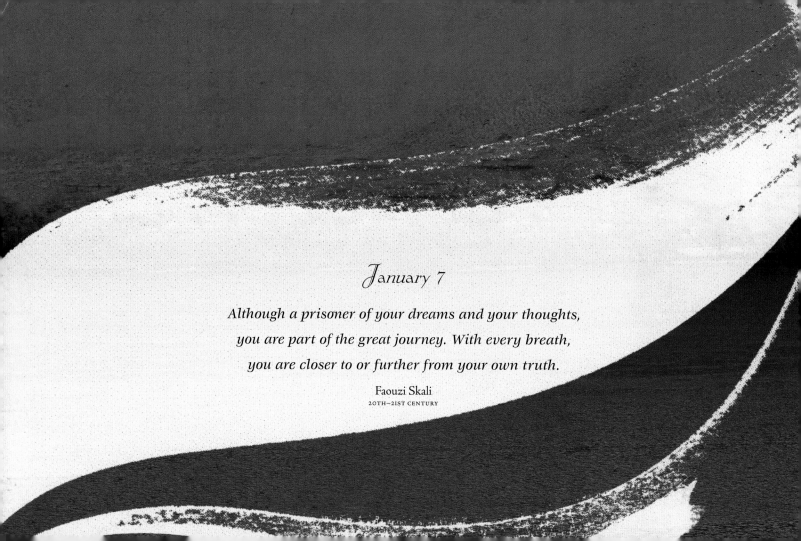

January 7

Although a prisoner of your dreams and your thoughts,
you are part of the great journey. With every breath,
you are closer to or further from your own truth.

Faouzi Skali
20TH–21ST CENTURY

Talk of tomorrow is not one of the conditions of the path.

Rumi
13TH CENTURY

On the far western edge of China, the Uighur city of Kashgar boasts the largest market in Central Asia, a destination
for traders from Kazakhstan, Tajikistan, Kyrgyzstan, Afghanistan, Pakistan, and India.

In this high place of yourself, the moment is no longer something we measure; it is the first impulse that has drawn the circles of your existence throughout eternity.

Faouzi Skali
20TH–21ST CENTURY

The Mosque of Suleiman the Magnificent (Süleymaniye Camii) in Turkey is the largest mosque in Istanbul. Constructed between 1550 and 1557, it is renowned for its marvelous acoustics.

That which sings and contemplates in you is still dwelling within the bounds of that first moment which scattered the stars into space.

Kahlil Gibran
20TH CENTURY

Fatima, a nineteen-year-old Tuareg, in Ghadames, Libya.

Repent a day before your death—in other words, immediately—for you do not know when you will die.

The Talmud
(TRACTATE SHABBAT)

Inside the Temple of Isis, on the island of Philae near Aswan, Egypt.

Suffering has its joyous side, despair has its gentleness,

and death has a meaning.

Naguib Mahfouz
20TH CENTURY

Resting in the shade of the willow trees, in the oasis city of Kashgar in the heart of Central Asia on the western border of China.

*Life is veiled and hidden, even as your greater self is hidden and
veiled. Yet when Life speaks, all the winds become words;
and when she speaks again, the smiles upon your lips
and the tears in your eyes turn also into words.*

Kahlil Gibran
20TH CENTURY

A chance encounter in a village in the Jebel Haraz, Yemen.
OVERLEAF: The 24,757-foot-high (7,546-m) Mustagh Ata stands in the heart of Central Asia, between China, Afghanistan, and Pakistan.

January 14

Set your eyes on life's ephemera and you will see eternity.

Faouzi Skali
20TH–21ST CENTURY

There are many ways to search but the object of the search is always the same. Don't you see that the roads to Mecca are all different, one coming from Byzantium, the other from Syria, others running through land or sea? The roads are diverse, the goal, one . . .

Rumi
13TH CENTURY

In Essaouira, Morocco, during the important prayer marking the end of Ramadan.

My friend, you lost yourself along this path because it is not your own.

You followed the alleyways and avenues that others traveled because

they were bustling and you thought you knew them!

Faouzi Skali
20TH–21ST CENTURY

This archway in Leptis-Magna, Libya, once a great metropolis of the Roman Empire, serves as a reminder that the city was the birthplace of Emperor Septimius Severus.

A person must break with the illusion that his life has already been written and his path already determined.

Marc-Alain Ouaknin
20TH–21ST CENTURY

The capital of Berber culture, Ghadames, Libya, was designed to protect its inhabitants from the desert heat.

Elevate yourself above time and space:

leave the world and be a world unto yourself.

Mahmud Shabistari
13TH–14TH CENTURY

Sixty-five-year-old Arif, a fisherman from Al Hudaydah, Yemen, rests on his nets after returning from the day's fishing.

My heart can take on any form:
a meadow for gazelles, a cloister for monks,
A temple for idols, the Ka'ba for pilgrims,
the tablets of the Torah, the leaves of the Qur'an.
I believe in the religion of love whichever way its caravan turns;
love is my religion and my faith.

Ibn 'Arabi
12TH–13TH CENTURY

Dromedaries in the southern Sahara of Chad.

Faith is to man as the wind is to a sailing boat.

The helmsman cannot decide the direction or the force of the wind,

but he can manipulate his own sails.

And that can make an enormous difference.

The same wind that may kill a mariner who is inexperienced, rash, or

merely unlucky will bring another safe to harbor.

Amin Maalouf
20TH–21ST CENTURY

Even at night, the feluccas are a popular tourist activity in Aswan, Egypt.
OVERLEAF: At the edge of the Sahara, the dunes of Ghadames, Libya, are only a few miles from the Algerian and Tunisian borders.

January 21

Never ask directions from someone who knows the way,

or you will never be able to get lost.

Rabbi Nachman of Breslov
18TH–19TH CENTURY

If things speak to us, it is because we are open to them,
we perceive them, listen to them, and give them meaning.
If things keep quiet, if they no longer speak to us, it is because we are
closed (idolatrous), because this gift of meaning is absent,
and the world shows itself in a frozen, dead light.

Marc-Alain Ouaknin
20TH–21ST CENTURY

At the Sunday market in Ta'izz, Yemen.

Set your eyes on your death and
you will receive each breath of life as a gift.

Faouzi Skali
20TH–21ST CENTURY

The Muslim cemetery on the Mount of Olives faces the Old City of Jerusalem and the Dome of the Rock.

The physical world is a fulcrum by which to lift yourself up to the intelligible world. If there were no connection or correspondence between the two, the path to ascend would be closed.

al-Ghazali
11TH–12TH CENTURY

A Toubou desert musician in the Ennedi Mountains of Chad.

Do not think this path is the path of passivity.

You must be attentive and listen.

Being detached from your thoughts allows you to be more enlightened;

but so long as you have not yet contemplated reality, keep trying.

Faouzi Skali
20TH–21ST CENTURY

The Friday Beit al-Faqih market, one of the biggest in Yemen.

Between the world of spirit and the world of matter there is a pathway

that we tread as though we were half-asleep.

Kahlil Gibran
20TH CENTURY

Sunset over the Moroccan Atlas.

A rose is a secret garden where trees hide.

One hundred roses alike,

This one is unique.

Rumi
13TH CENTURY

A young Tajik shepherdess in the high mountain pasture of Chichiklik in the heart of Central Asia, between China, Afghanistan, and Pakistan.
OVERLEAF: For several centuries, Essaouira, Morocco, served as an outpost on the way to the Cape Verde Islands and the Equator.

January 28

Look for the answer in the same place that you found the question.

Rumi
13TH CENTURY

Stop the words now.

Open the window in the center of your chest,

And let the spirits fly in and out.

Rumi
13TH CENTURY

Near Umm al-Maa, a lake in the Saharan region of Awbari, Libya, the last oasis of the Wadi al-Ajal.

At the moment you entered this world,

A ladder was placed in front of you to allow you to escape.

First you were a mineral, then you became a plant,

Then you became an animal: how could you ignore it?

Then you were made into a man gifted with knowledge, reason, and faith;

Observe this body, drawn from dust: what perfection it has acquired!

When you have transcended the condition of manhood,

no doubt you will become an angel.

Then you will have done with this earth, your dwelling will be in heaven.

Go beyond the angelic condition, dive into this ocean,

So that the drop of water that is you can become a sea.

Rumi
13TH CENTURY

Five-year-old Fatima in Ghadames, Libya.

Go to your fields and your gardens, and you shall learn that it is the
pleasure of the bee to gather honey of the flower,
But it is also the pleasure of the flower to yield its honey to the bee.
For to the bee a flower is a fountain of life,
And to the flower a bee is a messenger of love,
And to both, bee and flower, the giving and the receiving of pleasure
is a need and an ecstasy.

Kahlil Gibran
20TH CENTURY

The lush mountains of Kyrgyzstan, in the heart of Central Asia.

Look at the weeping cloud! Watch the laughing garden!

Rumi
13TH CENTURY

Lake Umm al-Maa in Awbari, Libya, an oasis in the Saharan Wadi al-Ajal.

Pleasure is a freedom-song,

But it is not freedom.

It is the blossoming of your desires,

But it is not their fruit.

It is a depth calling unto a height,

But it is not the deep nor the high.

It is the caged taking wing,

But it is not space encompassed.

Ay, in very truth, pleasure is a freedom-song.

Kahlil Gibran
20TH CENTURY

Dancing on Id Kah Masjid Square during the Korban, the Feast of the Sacrifice, as two drums and oboes are played from the minaret of a mosque in Kashgar in Central Asia.

You are subtle and without mark,

you are hidden even from the hidden.

Rumi
13TH CENTURY

Three elders talk on a shady porch of the mosque in Zabid, Yemen.

Who among you does not
feel that his power to love is
boundless?

Kahlil Gibran
20TH CENTURY

In Bukhara, Uzbekistan.

The wind speaks not more sweetly to the giant oaks than to the least of all the blades of grass; and he alone is great who turns the voice of the wind into a song made sweeter by his own loving.

Kahlil Gibran
20TH CENTURY

A traditional home in the medina of Ghadames, Libya.

There is nothing in this world human beings do not seek: they explore the mountains and the hills, aspire to know what is in the sea and beneath the sea, in the most remote deserts. However, there is one thing people neglect and do not seek: the divinity that is within them.

Rabbi Zadok ha-Kohen of Lublin
19TH CENTURY

Eight-year-old Uisam Ali in Ghadames, Libya.

The world of the Heavenly Kingdom is an invisible world, hidden from most of humankind, whereas the physical world is immediately perceptible since it is known to everyone.

al-Ghazali
11TH–12TH CENTURY

The Masjid-e Imam, or Imam Mosque, in Isfahan, Iran, one of the most beautiful mosques in the world.

A handful says: "I was old,"

Another handful says: "I was young,"

Another handful of dust will say: "Stop there,

I was someone, who was himself, the son of somebody."

You are in awe, and suddenly Love comes

That says: "Come nearer, it's Me, the Eternal Living."

Rumi
13TH CENTURY

In the Old City of Jerusalem.

Sanctify your mouth through prayer and study. Sanctify your nostrils by the long breath of patience. Sanctify your ears by listening to words of wisdom. Sanctify your eyes by closing them to disagreeable sights.

Rabbi Nachman of Breslov
18TH–19TH CENTURY

Located in the heart of the medina in Marrakech, Morocco, the Bin Yusuf Madrasa is an ancient Islamic university.

February 10

Only those whose hearts have been conquered by love

know the secret language of the glance.

Faouzi Skali
20TH–21ST CENTURY

An encounter with a child from a poor village near Ta'izz, Yemen, where people survive by making charcoal.

Live every day as if you were

going to live one hundred years.

Live as if you were living the

last day of your life.

Proverb attributed to Ibn 'Arabi

12TH–13TH CENTURY

The entire Temple of Isis on the island of Philae, in Egypt,
was moved when the dam on the Nile was built.

All worldly things
Come with strings
Joy beauty brings
Of freedom sings.

Omar Khayyám
11TH–12TH CENTURY

Thanks to its isolated location in the Himalayas, the peaceful Hunza Valley, now in Pakistan, has been protected for centuries.

Try and be a sheet of paper with nothing on it
Be a spot of ground where nothing is growing,
Where something might be planted,
A seed, possibly from the Absolute.

Rumi
13TH CENTURY

In Berber country, irrigated gardens in the palm grove in Ghadames, Libya, the "pearl of the desert."

Without passion the world would not survive. No man would build a house, plant a tree, and take a wife.

The Talmud
(SHOHAR TOV 32)

Two art students at the Madrasa-ye Chahar Bagh, an Islamic school in Isfahan, Iran.

The eye apprehends the large as small. It sees the sun the size of a bowl, and the stars like silver-pieces scattered upon a carpet of azure.

al-Ghazali
11TH–12TH CENTURY

The palm grove in Ghadames, Libya.

O soul, the breeze of spring is coming, so that you may raise

your hand toward the rose garden.

Rumi
13TH CENTURY

Mantra, the daughter of Mehdi and Mah, a young couple on a trip to Isfahan, Iran.

No man can reveal to you aught but that which already lies half asleep

in the dawning of your knowledge.

Kahlil Gibran
20TH CENTURY

An ancient city between the Dead Sea and the Red Sea, Petra, now in Jordan, prospered in the sixth century B.C.E. thanks to the caravans carrying incense and spices between Egypt, Syria, South Arabia, and the Mediterranean.
OVERLEAF: Two Tuareg chatting before the camel race during a celebration in Ghat, Libya.

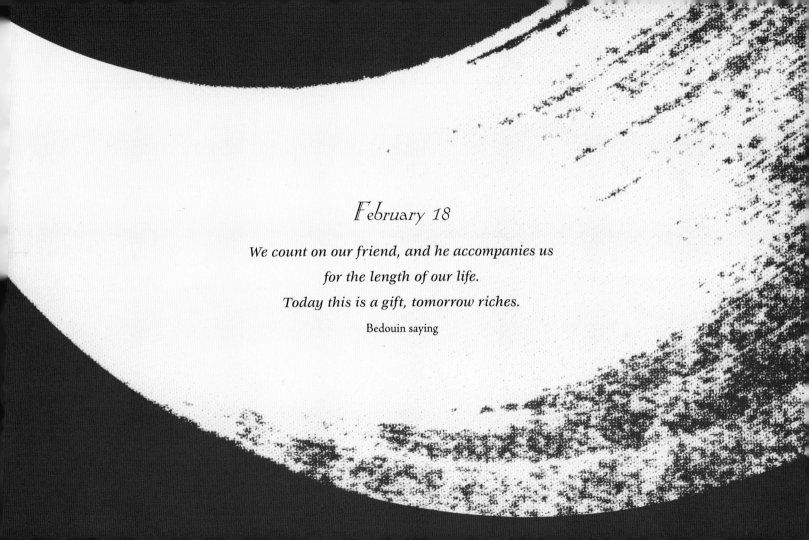

February 18

We count on our friend, and he accompanies us
for the length of our life.
Today this is a gift, tomorrow riches.

Bedouin saying

In your longing for your giant self lies your goodness:
and that longing is in all of you.
But in some of you that longing is a torrent rushing with might to the
sea, carrying the secrets of the hillsides and the songs of the forest.
And in others it is a flat stream that loses itself in angles and bends
and lingers before it reaches the shore.

Kahlil Gibran
20TH CENTURY

The lush mountains of Kyrgyzstan, in the heart of Central Asia.

Who dwells
at the core of my being?
I am calm itself
and he is the storm.

Hafiz
14TH CENTURY

Thirty-year-old Nasim at the Sunday market in Wadi Tabab, Yemen.

Daylight, full of small dancing particles

And the one great turning, our souls

Are dancing with you, without feet, they dance.

Can you see them when I whisper in your ear?

Rumi
13TH CENTURY

A sandstorm over the palm grove in Ghadames, Libya, a crossroads of trans-Saharan trade.

Like the shadow of a cypress tree in the meadow,

Like the shadow of a rose, I live

Close to the rose.

Rumi
13TH CENTURY

A contemplative walk at sunset along the Atlantic coast of Morocco.

Verily all things move within your being in constant half embrace,
the desired and the dreaded, the repugnant and the cherished,
the pursued and that which you would escape.

Kahlil Gibran
20TH CENTURY

Fourteen-year-old Lailah during a traditional celebration in Ghadames, Libya.

Wisdom is a view from on high, from the narrow path

between two precipices, two extreme ideas.

Amin Maalouf
20TH–21ST CENTURY

Sahara in Awbari, Libya.

February 25

Better to say: certainly, this is a reality, but the ultimate reality will always evade me.

Khaled Bentounès
20TH–21ST CENTURY

Mosaics at the Dome of the Rock, the third holiest Muslim site, in the Old City of Jerusalem.

The path that separates you from the garden of your desire,

my friend, is nowhere but in yourself.

It is as close and as far as you can be from yourself.

Faouzi Skali

20TH–21ST CENTURY

One of the side doors leading to the hall of prayer in Yeni Camii, Istanbul's "New Mosque."

With each breath you take you are in a new life,
and each is illumination or obscurity.

Faouzi Skali
20TH–21ST CENTURY

Gaotah, a sixteen-year-old Tuareg, in Ghadames, Libya.

What is it to cease breathing, but to free the breath from its restless tides, that it may rise and expand and seek God unencumbered?

Kahlil Gibran
20TH CENTURY

The top of one of the fortified towers that protected the city and harbor of Essaouira, Morocco, on the Atlantic coast.

Everything in this world—any event or person—is a touchstone intended to test your freedom of choice. Choose wisely.

Rabbi Nachman of Breslov
18TH–19TH CENTURY

A merchant's display of tea and beans at the souk in Sanaa, Yemen.

Lack of sincerity, my friend, turns you into a shadow. You live only for the image of yourself. What a strange spectacle to see a man driven by his shadow! Come, lift your eyes to the sun of Being and understand the source of truth and illusion. Do not remain a prisoner of the eyes of this world.

Faouzi Skali
20TH–21ST CENTURY

By the wall of the medina in the old city of Marrakech, Morocco.

Do not forget: you are never faced with a trial

that you cannot overcome.

Rabbi Nachman of Breslov
18H CENTURY

A villager from Chaghcharan, Afghanistan, brings fodder to the market.

March 4

Time is bright and dark,
war and cold in turns; make
not your abode save at the
fountainhead of time.

Rumi
13TH CENTURY

The Roman theater in Leptis-Magna, Libya.

Freedom of thought requires a climate of security. Otherwise we all cling to our certitudes and a ready-made vision of the world that stops us from thinking. For as long as we think, we question ourselves.

Philippe Yacine Demaison
20TH–21ST CENTURY

Ninety-year-old Muhammad al-Sakari in the old city of Sanaa, Yemen.

Unfortunately, today as always, people persist in holding fast to their individuality. They are afraid of disappearing if they recognize themselves in the other, their mirror and image.

Khaled Bentounès
20TH–21ST CENTURY

In a traditional house in Zabid, Yemen, where Pier Paolo Pasolini's *Arabian Nights* was filmed.

Universal love is the only possible standard for human relations.

Ben Azzai
2ND CENTURY C.E.

Eleven-year-old Rabia Oman in Ghadames, Libya, during the annual festival where Berber families celebrate their traditions.

The wine of the spirit frees you, my friend,
from your own weight. Like a bird freed from
its cage, your drunkenness expresses the
movement of the wings of your soul.

Faouzi Skali
20TH–21ST CENTURY

Seagulls await the return of fishermen to the port of Essaouira, Morocco.

The true miraculous crossing, for you,

would have the space of the world fade away.

And you could see the Beyond closer to you than even yourself.

Faouzi Skali
20TH–21ST CENTURY

Many Tuareg, such as this man on a camel, have given up the nomadic life to settle in cities, such as Ghadames, Libya, on the edge of the Sahara.

Do not frighten your soul with illusory fears:
draw the strength of your convictions from daily life.

Ahmad Muhammad Rami
20TH CENTURY

A mother and her three daughters inside a Mongolian yurt in the valleys of the High Altai, Mongolia.
OVERLEAF: A storm brewing in the Moroccan Atlas.

March 11

Would that you could live on the fragrance of the earth,

and like an air plant be sustained by the light.

Kahlil Gibran
20TH CENTURY

How can I tell you about it, my love? How can I describe the

state I was in before I loved you?

I had no yesterday to contemplate and no tomorrow to await.

Mursi Jamil 'Aziz
20TH CENTURY

Eight-year-old Aisha Ibrahim celebrating her traditions in Ghadames, Libya.

Nothing leads you along more than illusion.

Faouzi Skali
20TH–21ST CENTURY

Sunrise over the fishing port of Essaouira on Morocco's Atlantic coast.

Set your eyes on what you lack and your needs will be fulfilled.

Faouzi Skali
20TH–21ST CENTURY

In the Bin Yusuf Madrasa, in the heart of Marrakech's medina.

If it is a fear you would dispel, the seat of that fear is in your heart and not in the hand of the fear.

Kahlil Gibran
20TH CENTURY

Inside the Coptic monastery of Deir Anba Bishoi in Egypt.

It is to charge all things you fashion with a breath of your own spirit.

Kahlil Gibran
20TH CENTURY

Women in Ghadames weave during the festivities celebrating their traditions in Libya.

Your veils, my friend, are the habits you endlessly weave around yourself. The unknown frightens you, and you cannot cease from closing the gaps.

Faouzi Skali
20TH–21ST CENTURY

Dromedaries in the southern Sahara, Chad.

March 18

*Who is rich? The one who is
content with what he owns!*

Ben Zoma
2ND CENTURY

These totally veiled Hadramaut farm women in
Yemen wear a typical conical straw hat.

Do not tire of crying out with the joy of being alive

and you will hear no other cries.

Tuareg proverb

Praying in the Libyan desert.

At the heart of every winter, there is a quivering spring; and behind the veil of each night there is a smiling dawn.

Kahlil Gibran
20TH CENTURY

Ten-year-old Fatima in Ibb, Yemen.

Early in the morning, let me sing and wish the birds a good day.

The turtledoves and the greenfinches will sing along and answer me.

Mahmud Bayram al-Tunisi
20TH CENTURY

The Hunza Valley in the Himalayas, now in Pakistan.

You can never know a thing without knowing its opposite. You can never achieve sincerity without having experienced hypocrisy or having decided to struggle against it.

Khaled Bentounès, quoting Abu 'Uthman al-Maghribi
20TH–21ST CENTURY

The fortified granaries in the village of Nalut, in Libya, were used to store grain, jars of oil, and farm implements belonging to each family.

The deeper that sorrow carves into your being,

the more joy you can contain.

Kahlil Gibran
20TH CENTURY

Eighty-year-old Qartala at the Sunday market in Wadi Tabab, Yemen.

To imprison oneself in a victim mentality can do the injured party even more harm than the aggression itself. And this is as true of societies as of individuals. They huddle themselves away, they barricade themselves in, they try to ward everything off, they close their minds, they ruminate, they give up looking for anything new, they don't explore anymore, they don't make any more progress, they are afraid of the future, of the present, and of everyone else.

Amin Maalouf
20TH–21ST CENTURY

In the Ennedi Mountains of Chad in the southern Sahara.
OVERLEAF: A young bread vendor along the wall surrounding the Registan in Samarkand, Uzbekistan.

March 25

Your body is the harp of your soul,
And it is yours to bring forth sweet music from it or confused sounds.

Kahlil Gibran
20TH CENTURY

Each breath taken cannot be replaced and each imminent breath has its own particularity.

Faouzi Skali
20TH–21ST CENTURY

A young Tajik shepherdess in Central Asia, on the border of China, Afghanistan, and Pakistan.

And when you crush an apple with your teeth, say to it in your heart,

"Your seeds shall live in my body,

And the buds of your tomorrow shall blossom in my heart,

And your fragrance shall be my breath,

And together we shall rejoice through all the seasons."

Kahlil Gibran
20TH CENTURY

The Hunzakuts of the Hunza Valley in the Himalayas, now in Pakistan, are known for their longevity.

When you are with everyone but me, you're with no one.

When you are with no one but me, you're with everyone.

Instead of being so bound up with *everyone,* be *everyone.*

When you become that many, you're nothing.

Empty.

Rumi
13TH CENTURY

The courtyards of Nubian homes on the banks of the Nile in Egypt are shaded to protect their inhabitants from the intense heat.

It is in exchanging the gifts of the earth that you shall find abundance and be satisfied. Yet unless the exchange be in love and kindly justice, it will but lead some to greed and others to hunger.

Kahlil Gibran
20TH CENTURY

The oasis of Wadi al-Ajal, near Lake Umm al-Maa, in the Saharan region of Awbari, Libya.

When you are near me, I rediscover that paradise where my mind and my eyes take pleasure; your gaze is magic and inspiration.
Your smile is the joy of two hearts that live with shining hope.

Ahmad Muhammad Rami, sung by Umm Kulthum
20TH CENTURY

Nineteen-year-old Tisha in traditional dress in Ghadames, Libya.

*Let your board stand an altar on which the pure and the innocent
of forest and plain are sacrificed for that which is purer and
still more innocent in man.*

Kahlil Gibran
20TH CENTURY

A meal of welcome in Bukhara, Uzbekistan.
OVERLEAF: A peasant stops to pray on the way to Kashgar, Uighur, a city on the far western edge of China.

April 1

Where is God? Any place you let him in.

Rabbi Menachem Mendel of Kotsk
19TH CENTURY

They say that, when I was born,
my mother taught me to suck the milk.
And every night beside my crib
she taught me to sleep as soft as silk.
With a smile she pressed her lips to mine
till my mouth with joy overspilt.
She took my hand and guided my foot
till I learned to walk with a happy lilt.
One word, two words, then three and more—
that's how she taught me to talk.
That's why my life is part of her life
and will remain so as long as I live.

Iraj Mirza
19TH–20TH CENTURY

A child sleeping on his mother's lap on an Istanbul sidewalk.

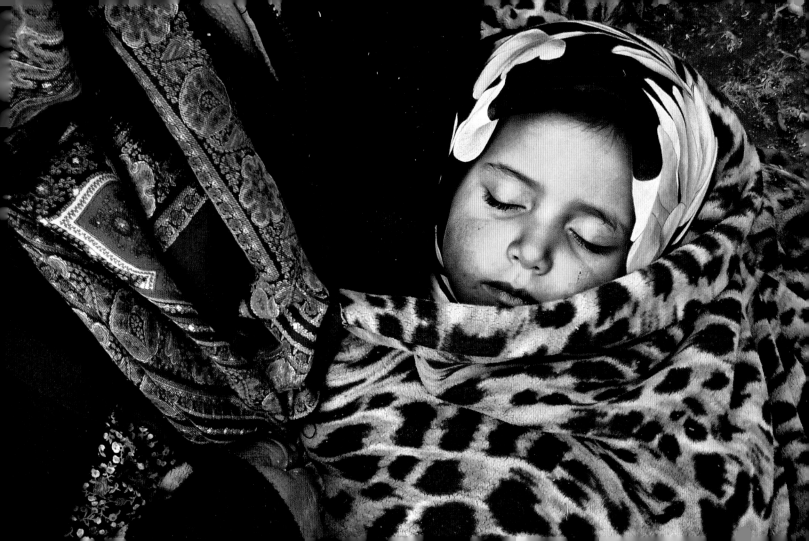

If I have the gift of prophecy and can fathom all mysteries and all

knowledge, and if I have a faith that can move mountains,

but have not love, I am nothing.

Saint Paul
(I COR. 13:2)

A solitary date tree in Awbari, Libya, in the Sahara region.

Every blessing on the house comes from the woman.

The Talmud

Fatima Ebayd Muhammad, a twenty-seven-year-old Nubian mother in Egypt.

My love, I was made for you, only for you.

And my heart lived with your tenderness, only for you.

Life is sweet, sweet are the dreams, how sweet! All that, only for you.

Ahmad Shafiq Kamal
20TH CENTURY

Inside a Mongolian yurt in the valleys of the High Altai, Mongolia.

And what desert greater shall there be, than that which lies in the courage and the confidence, nay the charity, of receiving?

Kahlil Gibran
20TH CENTURY

A resident of Ghadames tells the story of the old city, one of the most ancient in Libya.

You may give them your love but not your thoughts,

for they have their own thoughts.

Kahlil Gibran
20TH CENTURY

In Kashgar, a Uighur city on the far western edge of China.

Play with them for seven years,
educate them for seven years, and
be their friend for seven years.

Hadith

Four boys participating in the three-day festivities in
Ghadames, Libya, that celebrate their Berber traditions.

Hear the wordless subtleties,

and understand what catches not the understanding.

Rumi

13TH CENTURY

Many residents of the city of Tripoli, in Libya, come to experience the desert on the dunes of Ghadames.

This is how the world was created: everyone must know how to give and also to receive. Whoever does not know how to do one as well as the other is like a barren tree.

Rabbi Yitzchak Aisik the Hasid
19TH CENTURY

In the old city of Ibb, Yemen.

*The most precious friend is one who enchants you when he is with you
and speaks highly of you when you are apart.
He forgets offenses and is magnanimous in the face of injustice.
How delightful to have such a friend!*

Abu Hayyan al-Tawhidi
10TH–11TH CENTURY

Nasir, a Bedouin camel driver in Petra, Jordan.

If not now, when?

Hillel the Elder
1ST CENTURY B.C.E.—1ST CENTURY C.E.

A fisherman rests in the port of Al Hudaydah, Yemen, after his return from fishing on the Red Sea.

Forget not that the earth delights to feel your bare feet and the winds long to play with your hair.

Kahlil Gibran
20TH CENTURY

Lake Umm al-Maa in the Wadi al-Ajal, Libya.

You who have filled my life with love, I give you my life.

Ahmad Muhammad Rami
20TH CENTURY

Fatima Ebayd Muhammed, a twenty-seven-year-old Nubian mother, with her oldest son, Muhammad, four years old.
OVERLEAF: Naqsh-e Jahan Square, one of the most impressive in the world, and the Masjid-e Imam in Isfahan, Iran.

April 15

When "I" and "Thou" are absent, I don't know if this is a mosque, a synagogue, a church, or a temple.

Mahmud Shabistari
13–14TH CENTURY

You are both water and stream and are seeking for water.

Rumi
13TH CENTURY

Alexandra, a young Christian woman, prays during her Easter pilgrimage to Jerusalem.

Should you sit upon a cloud you would not see the boundary lines

between one country and another,

not the boundary stone between a farm and a farm.

It is a pity you cannot sit upon a cloud.

Kahlil Gibran
20TH CENTURY

An oasis in the Dadès region of the Moroccan Atlas.

Your children are not your children.

They are the sons and daughters of Life's longing for itself.

They come through you but not from you,

and though they are with you they belong not to you.

Kahlil Gibran
20TH CENTURY

A happy encounter in a village in the Jebel Haraz, Yemen.

Is not religion all deeds and all reflection?

Kahlil Gibran
20TH CENTURY

The watermelon market in Samarkand, Uzbekistan.

The great contradiction in man is that he wants the multiple but without wishing to pay the ransom of this sundering; he wants relativity with its savor of absoluteness or infinity, but without the suffering arising from its sharp edges; he desires extension but not limitation, as if the former could exist apart from the latter and as if pure extension could be found on the plane of measurable things.

Frithjof Schuon
20TH CENTURY

Inside the Temple of Pharaoh Ramses III in Luxor, Egypt.

Good and evil, our moral prison,
Joy and sorrow passing like season,
Fate in the way of logic and reason
Is the victim of far worse treason.

Omar Khayyám
11TH–12TH CENTURY

The village of Al-Muthmar al-Sufli, perched high in the Haraz mountains, Yemen.
OVERLEAF: A group of friends at the end of Ramadan in Essaouira, Morocco.

April 22

For without words, in friendship, all thoughts, all desires, all
expectations are born and shared with joy that is unacclaimed.

Kahlil Gibran
20TH CENTURY

All the souls are one. Each soul is a spark from the original soul, and this spark is inherent in all the other sparks, in the same way that our soul is inherent in every limb of our body.

Rabbi Shmuel Shmelke of Nikolsburg
18TH CENTURY

In Essaouira, Morocco, the crowd scatters after the great prayer marking the end of Ramadan.

You would rise in fancy unto the cloud, and you deem it height;
and you would pass over the vast sea and claim it to be distance.
But I say unto you that when you sow a seed in the earth,
you reach a greater height; and when you hail the beauty of the
morning to your neighbor, you cross a greater sea.

Kahlil Gibran
20TH CENTURY

The city of Sanaa, the capital of Yemen, a UNESCO World Heritage site considered one of the most remarkable urban landscapes in the world.

When you are joyous, look deep into your heart, and you shall find it is only that which has given you sorrow that is giving you joy.

Kahlil Gibran
20TH CENTURY

An encounter with a child from a poor village near Ta'izz, Yemen.

You are water, I am a stream; how should I seek to join you? The stream has no luster if you do not open the water.

Rumi
13TH CENTURY

Fatima Ebayd Mohamed, a twenty-seven-year-old Nubian mother, in the courtyard of her home near the Nile in Egypt.

If you would know God be not therefore a solver of riddles.

Rather look about you and you shall see Him

playing with your children.

–Kahlil Gibran
20TH CENTURY

At the Friday Beit al-Faqih market, one of the liveliest markets in Yemen.

The fulfilled man exists in a permanent and natural way: a harmonious balance in his relationship with the infinitely small and the infinitely large, in other words, with the microcosm and the macrocosm.

Khaled Bentounès
20TH–21ST CENTURY

Ceramics in the Bagh-e Tarikhi-ye Fin gardens in Kashan, Iran.
OVERLEAF: Lake Umm al-Maa in the Wadi al-Ajal in Libya.

April 29

*Love is the fusion of sky and earth, of past and future, of song and
dance; it is the fulfillment of their complementary nature.*

Kahlil Gibran
20TH CENTURY

Remember that you are not alone in the world. You depend on a thousand creatures that sustain the fabric of your life. The mirror of your heart is permeated with a multitude of images. Your soul is like a feather carried by the winds. But much more is still needed before you see yourself as you are.

Faouzi Skali
20TH–21ST CENTURY

A Palestinian in the Old City of Jerusalem.

The hand opens, spreads its fingers outward.

But when it reaches the world, the fingers do not close in a tight grip.

The fingers remain extended, offered.

And so the hand becomes a caress.

Marc-Alain Ouaknin
20TH–21ST CENTURY

In Ghadames, Libya, where Berber and Tuareg families celebrate their heritage.

You plant the tree of hope and
water it in the shade of the garden of my love.
All that you love in this world, I love too.

Ahmad Muhammad Rami, sung by Umm Kulthum
20TH CENTURY

The traditional family home of Bashir Yunus in the medina of Ghadames, Libya.

It is not the eyes that are blind, but the hearts.

The Qur'an
(22.46)

At the Berber and Tuareg festivities in Ghadames, Libya.

To pray is much more than reciting a prayer. The heart, the muscles, and bones of your being must be intensely taut; the soul must be purified, and forgiveness must wholly inhabit your consciousness. We must get rid, so to speak, of all materiality and increase our intellectual powers as much as is possible. Then the words will come by themselves, as if they were in you since the creation of the world, as if it were the last step in a process and these words did not belong to you. You must pray within yourself before you address the heavens.

Rabbi Hanina ben Dosa
1ST CENTURY C.E.

A Moroccan villager prays on his way to the well.

The pearls of wisdom, my friend, rest in the depths of your soul.

Faouzi Skali
20TH–21ST CENTURY

Father Luc Ambabul, a Coptic monk, on the grounds of the isolated monastery of Saint Paul of Thebes in Egypt.
OVERLEAF: In Aswan, Egypt, the feluccas once used to transport merchandise on the Nile are now used mostly for tourism.

May 6

Life and death are one, even as the river and the sea are one.

Kahlil Gibran
20TH CENTURY

Listen to the birth of this ray of honey within you.
Let yourself be caught in the net of its charms,
let it reveal to you what no ear has heard, what no eye has seen,
what no imagination has conceived.

Faouzi Skali
20TH–21ST CENTURY

Ten-year-old Sanajadih, in traditional dress, in Ghadames, Libya.

The chains of the world exist nowhere but within you.

Protect yourself from your own tricks, and the demon itself will give up

the battle for lack of allies.

Faouzi Skali
20TH–21ST CENTURY

The Friday Beit al-Faqih market, one of the most important in Yemen.

I do not have one personality, I have several.

Orhan Pamuk
20TH–21ST CENTURY

The Berber celebrations in Ghadames, Libya.

If in your thought you must measure time into seasons,

let each season encircle all the other seasons.

Kahlil Gibran
20TH CENTURY

Originally grown in Persia and Turkey, the tulip was celebrated with sumptuous feasts in the eighteenth century. In Istanbul in the spring, it returns to the limelight.

May this hand

in which the spirit has huddled

be full of seed.

Edmond Jabès
20TH CENTURY

Hana, the four-year-old granddaughter of Ali Khalib, in the village of Manakha, Yemen.

To be idle is to become a stranger unto the seasons,
and to step out of life's procession, that marches in majesty
and proud submission towards the infinite.

Kahlil Gibran
20TH CENTURY

Ornamented wall in Marrakech's Dar M'Nebhi Palace, which has been converted into a museum of contemporary art.

May 13

Plunge into the ocean of your heart, for there you will find the universe.

'Attar
12TH–13TH CENTURY

The Tamlelt cliff hangs over the Dadès River as it flows down from the limestone plateaus of the central High Atlas in Morocco.

Your god-self dwells not alone in your being. Much in you is still man,

and much in you is not yet man.

Kahlil Gibran
20TH CENTURY

View of Sanaa, Yemen, a UNESCO World Heritage site celebrated for its remarkable urban landscape.

Listen, my friend, to that song deep within you with which the essence of beauty calls to you.

Faouzi Skali
20TH–21ST CENTURY

A girl with her grandmother at the Berber festivities in Ghadames, Libya.

And before you leave the marketplace, see that no one has gone his way with empty hands.

Kahlil Gibran
20TH CENTURY

Built in 1660, the Egyptian bazaar in Istanbul, Turkey, is full of spices and alluring aromas.

Set your eyes on your cruelty and He will soften you with

His Compassion.

Faouzi Skali

20TH–21ST CENTURY

The Church of the Holy Savior in Chora (Kariye Müzesi) in Istanbul boasts some of the most beautiful frescoes and mosaics in the Byzantine world.

If we considered the Divine in every act or project we carried out, we would place ourselves within a universal perspective in which nobody would be harmed. For God is omnipresent. He is alive in human beings as well as in animals, the Moon, the Sun, and all the galaxies in this marvelous and harmonious movement that is life.

Khaled Bentounès
20TH–21ST CENTURY

A believer prays during the Korban, the Feast of the Sacrifice, in Kashgar, a Uighur city in Central Asia.

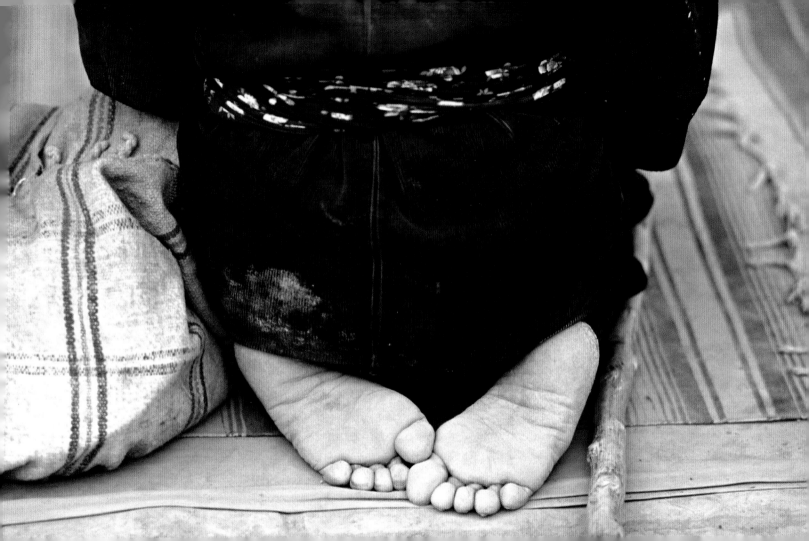

There is something better than good: the one who does good.

Arab proverb

Sanaa's souk in Yemen is one of the oldest markets on the Arabian Peninsula.
OVERLEAF: In the heart of Central Asia, the Tien Shan mountain range divides eastern Kyrgyzstan from China.

May 20

Even if God exists, man must first of all behave as if He did not.

Rabbi Nachman of Breslov
18TH–19TH CENTURY

You often say, "I would give, but only to the deserving."

The trees in your orchard say not so, nor the flocks in your pasture.

They give that they may live, for to withhold is to perish.

Kahlil Gibran
20TH CENTURY

When the ground is too arid in Morocco, goats climb the argan tree to nibble at its leaves.

One good word is enough warmth for a whole winter.

Arab proverb

Thirteen-year-old Tahir, a young fisherman from Al Hudaydah, Yemen, on the Red Sea.

It is well to give when asked, but it is better to give unasked,

through understanding.

Kahlil Gibran
20TH CENTURY

In the old city of Ghadames, Libya, which is located on an important trans-Saharan trade route.

If you lack wisdom, what do you possess?

If you acquire wisdom, what are you lacking?

Midrash

In the port of Al Hudaydah, Yemen, on the Red Sea, Arif, a sixty-five-year-old fisherman, rests after his return from the day's fishing.

In your heart there are many other gazes, so many false gods for whom you try to make yourself more beautiful. You waste precious time and energy even though you think you are doing the right thing.

Faouzi Skali
20TH–21ST CENTURY

Lamps for sale near Djemaa el-Fna Square in Marrakech, Morocco.

Is not dread of thirst when your well is full

the thirst that is unquenchable?

Kahlil Gibran
20TH CENTURY

Istanbul's Sultan Ahmed Mosque, known as the Blue Mosque, is adorned with six minarets whose slender design is characteristic of Ottoman architecture.
OVERLEAF: The harbor of Agadir, Morocco's leading port for sardines.

May 27

Money breeds madness.

Rabbi Nachman of Breslov
18TH–19TH CENTURY

The door that does not open for charity will open for the doctor.

Jewish proverb

A typical front door of a casbah, near Tizirt, Morocco.

Whether fortune smiles on you or not, whether your days are happy or unhappy, your lives are a perpetual exchange: there is no joy or sorrow that does not serve to prove your sincerity, to strengthen your bonds as well as your support for one another.

Abu Hayyan al-Tawhidi
10TH–11TH CENTURY

Two villagers from Chaghcharan, Afghanistan, talk in the shade of the willows.

When you give from your assets, you give very little;

when you give of yourself, then the gift is real.

Kahlil Gibran
20TH CENTURY

An inhabitant of the port of Al Hudaydah, Yemen, on the Red Sea heads home with lunch for his family.

Certain actions free your heart of its maladies.

The generosity of giving frees you from greed.

The gift you can make of yourself each moment

frees you from yourself.

All that remains, my friend, is what you give.

Faouzi Skali
20TH–21ST CENTURY

Bedouin women in Petra, Jordan, carry on their ancestral way of life.

Beauty is life when life unveils her holy face.

But you are life and you are the veil.

Beauty is eternity gazing at itself in a mirror.

But you are eternity and you are the mirror.

All your hours are wings that beat through space from self to self.

Kahlil Gibran
20TH CENTURY

The Tuareg of Libya are often called the "blue people," after the color of their *cheche* head wear, which are dyed with indigo.

Giving is unique to human beings. It's one of the traits that radically distinguishes us from the animal world.
Charity is thus a line of demarcation between the humanity that inhabits us and the animality that possesses us.

Philippe Yacine Demaison
20TH–21ST CENTURY

An old man rests in the Al-Abhar Mosque in the old city of Sanaa, Yemen.
OVERLEAF: In the Himalayan Hunza Valley in Pakistan, the Hunzakuts claim direct descent from Alexander the Great.

June 3

All you have shall some day be given;
Therefore give now, that the seasons of giving may be yours and not
your inheritors'.

Kahlil Gibran
20TH CENTURY

My words are meat to the angels; if I speak no words, the hungry angels say, "Speak, why are you silent?"

Rumi
13TH CENTURY

A Tuareg man in Libya sitting on a traditional forked-horn camel saddle.

Show me your eyes; let them wander in the universe of my own. Give me your hands; let them rest in the caresses of my own.

Ahmad Shafiq Kamal
20TH CENTURY

A child from a poor village near Ta'izz, Yemen.

Have you peace, the quiet urge that reveals your power?

Kahlil Gibran
20TH CENTURY

The mounted tourist police provide security for visitors to Petra, Jordan.

If your tongue endlessly speaks of peace, think above all about what your heart conveys. First, try to receive the gift that you want to give.

Faouzi Skali
20TH–21ST CENTURY

Fatima in the courtyard of her home in the village of Garb Sehel, Egypt.

Every creature honor and respect

Bird or beast, plant or insect

If you look at life you will detect

From dust to dust, divine intellect.

Omar Khayyám
11TH–12TH CENTURY

Muhammad al-Ansi, a merchant in Sanaa's souk, which is one of the oldest markets on the Arabian Peninsula.

He who wears his morality as his best garment were better naked.

Kahlil Gibran
20TH CENTURY

The Sahara Desert in Awbari, Libya.
OVERLEAF: Residents of Tripoli come to experience the desert on the dunes of Ghadames, Libya.

June 10

Let us always question the sincerity of our intention before

transforming it into action.

Khaled Bentounès
20TH–21ST CENTURY

It is not the world that is the site of the question,

but the question that is the site of the world.

Rabbi Nachman of Breslov
18TH–19TH CENTURY

Ghadames, Libya, the capital of Berber culture.

An idea becomes false the moment we are satisfied with it.

Marc-Alain Ouaknin
20TH–21ST CENTURY

Smoking the narghile (here in Egypt) is a common social activity throughout the Arab Middle East.

A being capable of a destiny other than his own is a fertile soul.

Rabbi Elisha ben Abuyah
1ST CENTURY C.E.

Thirty-four-year-old Muhammad Wasim at the Beit al-Faqih market in Yemen.

"Knowing the world too well"—the belief in a preconceived definition of the world and one's fate—is an obstacle to human freedom.

Marc-Alain Ouaknin
20TH–21ST CENTURY

Hieroglyphics detail at the temple of Pharaoh Ramses III in the Valley of the Kings, Luxor, Egypt.

The further science progresses the more man is bound to ponder the purpose of his own existence.

Amin Maalouf
20TH–21ST CENTURY

At the souk in Sanaa, Yemen.

June 16

Despite the materialism of our modern century and the infernal noise
of its mechanical, industrial, nuclear, and military power, there still
exist a few representatives of that superior type of humanity who in
silence inquire, meditate, and pray.

Khaled Bentounès
20TH–21ST CENTURY

A Jewish man prays near the Western Wall in Jerusalem's Old City.

*You must go beyond all that
you see behind or ahead of you
by going beyond yourself.*

'Attar
12TH–13TH CENTURY

The final prayer marking the end of Ramadan in Essaouira, Morocco.

All that one thinks does not deserve to be said.

And all that one says does not deserve to be written.

And all that one writes does not deserve to be printed.

Rabbi Menachem Mendel of Kotsk
19TH CENTURY

In Jibla, Yemen, a villager reads the Qur'an in the old Queen Arwa Mosque.

When you look at the world, you look at the Creator.

Baal Shem Tov
18TH CENTURY

A young Tajik girl in the high mountain pasture of Chichiklik in Central Asia.

Set your eyes on your ignorance

and a mountain of knowledge will be given you.

Faouzi Skali

20TH–21ST CENTURY

Reading the Qur'an at a madrasa, an Islamic school, in Ghadames, Libya.

The fool says what he knows; the wise man knows what he says.

Rabbi Simcha Bunim of Pshiskha
18TH–19TH CENTURY

A Tajik camel driver in Mustagh Ata, located in Central Asia near China, Afghanistan, and Pakistan.

Against envy, refresh your eye at the source of the gift.

Against avidity, cultivate a grateful heart.

Against the desire for fame, the quest for an obscure life.

Faouzi Skali
20TH–21ST CENTURY

Father David silently reads his prayer book in the Coptic monastery of Deir Anba Bishoi in Egypt.

Truth is not what the tongue articulates. If you want to know what it
is, listen as it comes to you, in waves, from the depths of your being.
For it is from this inner necessity that the vision is born.

Faouzi Skali
20TH–21ST CENTURY

Twelve-year-old Safaa Gamal, of Nubian ancestry, lives with her family on the banks of the Nile in Egypt.
OVERLEAF: In the Ennedi Massif of Chad, in the southern Sahara, dromedaries are lead to a watering hole.

June 24

The true path to deliverance is humility.

Faouzi Skali
20TH–21ST CENTURY

Teaching is found in the continuous movement between what has already been said and what remains to be said—what is being said differently.

Marc-Alain Ouaknin
20TH–21ST CENTURY

A primary school in the Hunza Valley of the Himalayas in Pakistan.

If you feel more important than many human beings, think of only one thing your entire life: releasing your soul from this malady.

Faouzi Skali
20TH–21ST CENTURY

The statue of Ramses II, which used to stand before the columns of the Temple of Gerf Hussein, illuminated by the projectors of the Nubian Museum in Aswan, Egypt.

All day and night, music,

A quiet, bright

Reedsong. If it

Fades, we fade.

Ibn 'Arabi
12TH–13TH CENTURY

At the foot of Mustagh Ata (24,757 ft; 7,546 m) in the heart of Central Asia, between China, Afghanistan, and Pakistan.

And for the open-handed the search for one who shall receive

is joy greater than giving.

Kahlil Gibran
20TH CENTURY

A happy greeting in a village near Ta'izz, Yemen.

Everything that comes from the ego can only lead us astray.
It is a false pretense to think God's approval can be earned the way
we earn our daily bread, through prayer, study, or generosity.
God cannot be earned. He is discovered in the attitude of
humility, simplicity, and letting go.

Khaled Bentounès
20TH—21ST CENTURY

The beautiful Masjid-e Imam, also known as the Masjid-i Shah (Shah Mosque), in Isfahan, Iran.

Violence is believing that we already

have knowledge of the Other and the world.

Marc-Alain Ouaknin
20TH–21ST CENTURY

Bas-relief detail of the Roman theater at Sabrata, Libya.
OVERLEAF: The wind blows sand across the southern Sahara in Chad.

July 1

What good is it for a man to gain the whole world, and yet lose or forfeit his very self?

Saint Luke
(LUKE 9:25)

Set your eyes on your weakness and you will be strengthened.

Faouzi Skali
20TH–21ST CENTURY

Situated in an oasis, the city of Ghadames, Libya, is called the "pearl of the desert."

The wise replace pride with humility, jealousy with generosity, vanity with sincerity, hate with love, and confusion with serenity. Their secret is revealed not in the rules of the perceptible world, but those of the spirit.

Faouzi Skali
20TH–21ST CENTURY

This young Italian monk reads Easter prayers in front of the Church of the Holy Sepulchre in Jerusalem's Old City.

God formed man from the dust of the earth. He blew into his nostrils

the breath of life, and man became a living being.

The Bible
(GENESIS)

Ten-year-old Taman, a Bedouin girl, selling striated rocks in a cave in Petra, Jordan.

Let me declare, without allegory:
we are puppets of our master, toys
on the Table of Existence, one by one
Sent back to the toy chest of Non-Existence.

Omar Khayyám
11TH–12TH CENTURY

The Sultan Ahmed Mosque in Istanbul, Turkey, known as the Blue Mosque because its interior walls are decorated with blue tiles.

Submission to God entails the notions of peace, wisdom, and tolerance.

To submit does not mean to renounce, but to exist.

This attitude bestows on individuals who address God directly a sense

of their own responsibilities.

Tahar Ben Jelloun
20TH–21ST CENTURY

Ceramic tile decoration inside Lotfollah Mosque in Isfahan, Iran.

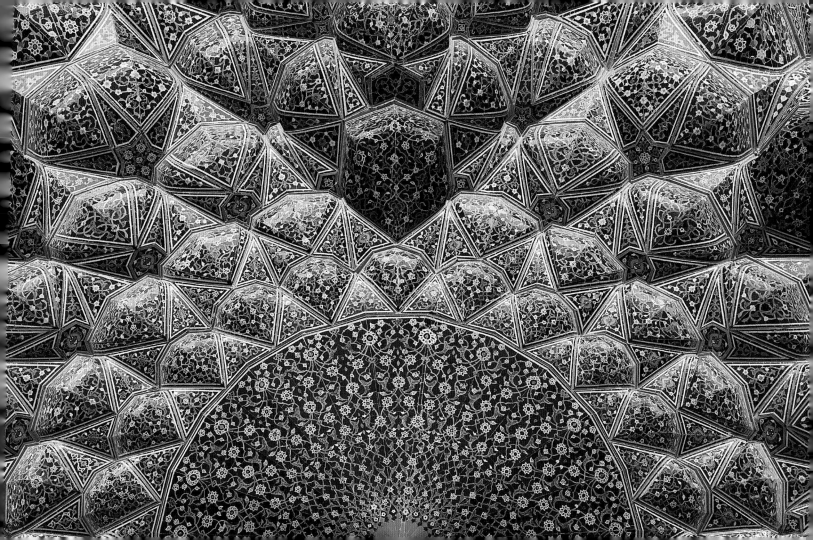

This is love: to disregard this world,

to see only that which you yourself have seen.

Rumi

13TH CENTURY

Ten-year-old Sanajadih in Ghadames, Libya.
OVERLEAF: Al Khazneh (Treasury) in Petra, Jordan, is a tomb entirely carved out of the rock.

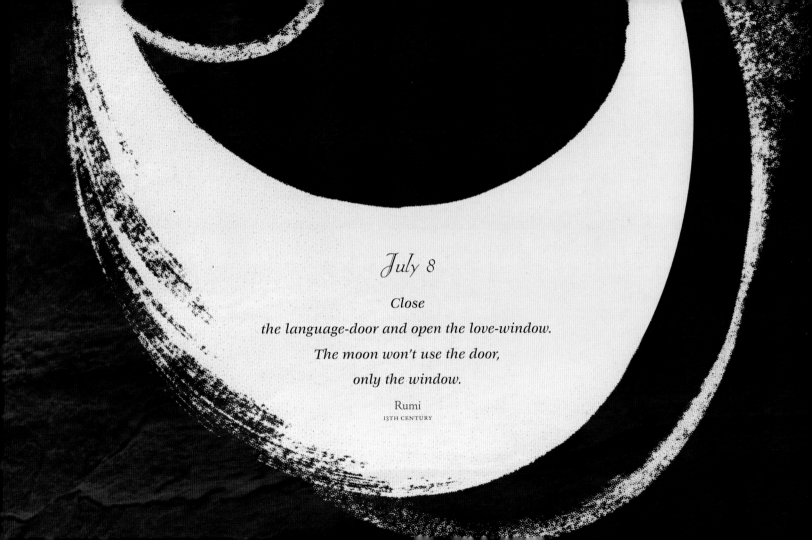

July 8

Close
the language-door and open the love-window.
The moon won't use the door,
only the window.

Rumi
13TH CENTURY

Whoever does not increase his knowledge diminishes it.

Hillel the Elder
1ST CENTURY B.C.E.–1ST CENTURY C.E.

Reading the Qur'an in the madrasa, or Islamic school, in Libya.

To call the world into question, to shake up our knowledge of the world,

is Revelation.

Marc-Alain Ouaknin
20TH—21ST CENTURY

Camels drinking from a water hole in the Sahara in Chad.

For Muhammad, the teachings were based on the Word; for Jesus, on Love; for Moses, on the Law. Starting from the Light, each prophet gave it a particular accent. Why? In Creation, no two things are identical.

Khaled Bentounès
20TH–21ST CENTURY

The Marrakech "garden of rare essences" by Jacques Majorelle, a French master of Art Nouveau.

When the canary made its way to the field

Found the rose and wine smiling, kneeled,

In tongues its message in my ear it thus reeled

Hark, no moment in time did twice yield.

Omar Khayyám
IITH–I2TH CENTURY

Alma Fakhre Mecattaf, a Lebanese writer fighting for women's rights.

*Peace will no longer be limited to your thoughts. It will inhabit the
depths of your heart and accompany each of your actions.*

Faouzi Skali
20TH–21ST CENTURY

A worshipper crosses the courtyard of the Al-Sunna Mosque in Jibla, Yemen, on his way to prayer.

One can accumulate facts, but one does not always achieve Knowledge.

To know, one must be "awake" to the Living.

Khaled Bentounès
20TH–21ST CENTURY

An open-air barber in Kashgar, a Uighur city in Sinkiang province at the western border of China.
OVERLEAF: On the first dunes of the Sahara, at the borders of Algeria, Tunisia, and Libya.

July 15

My rule is to receive you with hospitality and to let you go in peace.

A desert hermit

Disputes between men stem from names, my friend;

Should they reach meanings, then peace would descend.

Rumi
13TH CENTURY

The shofar, or ram's horn, is blown in a synagogue in Israel to announce the end of the fast on Yom Kippur.

If, despite your desire to be happy, you should hit bottom,
reclaim the strength you found in happier times.
It is not impossible that joy will return.

Rabbi Nachman of Breslov
18TH–19TH CENTURY

Tafraout, a small Berber town in the Atlas Mountains of Morocco.

If your leaders say to you, "Look, the kingdom is in the sky,"
then the birds of the sky will precede you. If they say, "It is in the sea,"
then the fish will precede you. Rather, the kingdom is within you
and it is outside you.

Saint Thomas
(THE GOSPEL OF THOMAS 3:1–3)

A young Tajik girl in the high mountain pasture of Chichiklik near the borders of China, Afghanistan, and Pakistan.

For that which is boundless in you abides in the mansion of the sky,
whose door is the morning mist, and whose windows are the songs
and the silences of night.

Kahlil Gibran
20TH CENTURY

The mosque in Ghadames, Libya.

For thought is a bird of space, that in a cage of words may indeed unfold its wings but cannot fly.

Kahlil Gibran
20TH CENTURY

A bird market in the city of Kashgar in Western China

Say not, "I have found the truth," but rather, "I have found a truth."

Say not, "I have found the path of the soul." Say rather, "I have met the

soul walking upon my path."

For the soul walks upon all paths.

The soul walks not upon a line, neither does it grow like a reed.

The soul unfolds itself, like a lotus of countless petals.

Kahlil Gibran
20TH CENTURY

Father Thomas, a peaceful Coptic monk, in the monastery of Saint Bishoi in Wadi Natrun, Egypt.
OVERLEAF: The monastic compound built to house the monks on the heights of the isolated Coptic monastery of Saint Paul of Thebes (Deir Mar Boulos) in Egypt contains five churches.

July 22

If you ask, "Incarnation?" I will simply answer, "Light."

Shaykh Abu al-Hasan Kharaqani
10TH–11TH CENTURY

The best path, my friend, is a perpetual drunkenness.
Even if your external appearance remains sober, the cup of your soul
must always taste this wine of felicity. Only this, my friend, can
protect you from an inner drought.

Faouzi Skali
20TH–21ST CENTURY

Wadi al-Ajal in the Libyan Sahara.

See the fire beneath the ashes
reborn after an intimate gentleness
is forgotten.

Faouzi Skali
20TH–21ST CENTURY

Ten-year-old Rim in the medina of Ghadames, Libya.

Learn to accept your night and face your trouble with patience.
Not until the end of night does the dawn break, much as fruit sprouts
from the obscure belly of the earth.
The gift of night may be more favorable than that of light.

Faouzi Skali
20TH–21ST CENTURY

A tomato vendor grabs a nap in the shade of an alley in Kabul, Afghanistan.

Do not forget: things can go from

the worst to the best in the blink of an eye.

Rabbi Nachman of Breslov
18TH–19TH CENTURY

Stormy skies over the Atlas Mountains of Morocco.

Remember those tears without reason, the undefined sadness.
You probably did not know it, but your soul already aspired to its
uncommon image.

Faouzi Skali
20TH–21ST CENTURY

Aisulu, a young Kazakh shepherdess, whose name means "beauty of the moon," spends the summer living with her family in a yurt in the High Altai of Mongolia.

The mind can not encompass its description, for in it is the union of opposites, a composition without composition, amazing!— constrained yet with free will.

Rumi
13TH CENTURY

July 29

To know yourself is to live one hundred lives.

'Attar
12TH–13TH CENTURY

At rest near the mosque in the old city of Kashgar in Central Asia.

Every day one must dance, even if only in thought.

Rabbi Nachman of Breslov
18TH–19TH CENTURY

Puppet of a Sufi dancer in the window of a shop in the Grand Bazaar of Istanbul, Turkey.

The bird of the spirit resides
On a branch of light
In a clear space
At the peak of the universe.

Faouzi Skali
20TH–21ST CENTURY

An old school built in a palm grove in Ghadames, Libya, during the Italian colonial period.

When you are sorrowful look again in your heart, and you shall see that in truth you are weeping for that which has been your delight.

Kahlil Gibran
20TH CENTURY

A Hunzakut woman of the Hunza Valley in the Himalayas, in Pakistan.

Humor is the drunken truth.

George Nathan
20TH CENTURY

A Bactrian camel rests on the steppes of the High Altai in Mongolia.

Try to have only positive thoughts. They will work wonders in you.

Rabbi Nachman of Breslov
18TH–19TH CENTURY

The Lebanese feminist writer Alma Fakhre Mecattaf.

Of the good in you I can speak, but not of the evil.

For what is the evil but good tortured by its own hunger and thirst?

Kahlil Gibran
20TH CENTURY

The hull of a fishing boat in the harbor of Agadir, Morocco.

August 5

Only the absolute exists; the

temporal is ephemeral.

Khaled Bentounès
20TH–21ST CENTURY

Founded on the Mediterranean coast by the Phoenicians
in the seventh century B.C.E., Leptis-Magna in Libya
was a great metropolis of the Roman Empire.

Any true action must be driven by a devotion, a spiritual intention; this alone makes it a form of worship. In the same way, a spiritual attitude can lead to a free and effective action.

Faouzi Skali
20TH–21ST CENTURY

Women in Ghadames, Libya, spinning goat wool during traditional festivities held in the city.

Always look for what is good in you. Concentrate all your attention on
this good part of yourself, show it in the full light of day,
and transform depression into the joy of being.

Rabbi Nachman of Breslov
18TH–19TH CENTURY

Spring in bloom in the Hunza Valley, situated at 7,999 ft (2,438 m) above sea level, in Pakistan.

Work is great, for it honors the one who performs it.

Rabbi Shimon bar Yochai
2ND CENTURY C.E.

The production and sale of Moroccan carpets provides a living for hundreds of families and jobs for the country's women.

Your actions are certainly the fabric of your soul.

But do not rely on their appearance. For it is the intention behind your

actions that breathes life into them.

Faouzi Skali
20TH–21ST CENTURY

At prayer in Yeni Camii, the "New Mosque," in Istanbul.

If you need advice, work with Patience.

If you want to grow, make your way with Patience.

Yunus Emre
13TH CENTURY

A child in the medina, the old city of Tripoli, Libya.

Who can separate his faith from his actions,
or his belief from his occupations?
Who can spread his hours before him, saying,
"This for God and this for myself;
this for my soul, and this other for my body?"

Kahlil Gibran
20TH CENTURY

The delightful aroma of spices fills the Egyptian bazaar in Istanbul.

Build of your imaginings
a bower in the wilderness
ere you build a house
within the city walls.

Kahlil Gibran
20TH CENTURY

Tuaregs and their camels in the desert dunes
of Fezzan, south of Ghat in Libya.

We must be whole.

That is where the unity of being resides. The internal and external

must be perfectly and totally coordinated, in true symbiosis.

One cannot play with the Truth. If our intentions are not in keeping

with our actions, if we are hypocritical toward ourselves and others,

we are wasting our time. Our efforts and energies will be in vain.

Khaled Bentounès
20TH–21ST CENTURY

Salah 'Abduh al-Fatah relaxes by smoking the narghile at his home on the Nubian banks of the Nile in Egypt.

When you work you are a flute through whose heart the whispering

of the hours turns to music.

Kahlil Gibran
20TH CENTURY

Washing dishes in a stream in the remote Hunza Valley of Pakistan's Himalayan region.

I say that life is indeed darkness save when there is urge,

And all urge is blind save when there is knowledge,

And all knowledge is vain save when there is work,

And all work is empty save when there is love;

And when you work with love you bind yourself to yourself,

and to one another, and to God.

Kahlil Gibran
20TH CENTURY

A woman working clay at Tuareg festivities in Tunil, Libya.

Whoever has a soul catches the scent of the rose garden of the soul;

whoever has that realizes we are all that.

Rumi
13TH CENTURY

Ten-year-old Iman Sanusi 'Ali in Ghadames, Libya, during the annual Berber celebration.

What is it to work with love?

It is to weave the cloth with threads drawn from your heart,

even as if your beloved were to wear that cloth.

Kahlil Gibran
20TH CENTURY

A fisherman repairs his nets in the port of Agadir, Morocco.

Honor is not derived from the profession you practice: it is the person who gives value to the position he holds.

Rabbi Yose ben Halafta
2ND CENTURY C.E.

A sewing workshop in Tripoli's old city.

In the earth there are signs for

those who are sure,

And in your own souls too;

will you not see?

The Qur'an
(51.20)

Spring in the village of Abyaneh, Iran.

What you see is your face.

What you think of someone is what you think of yourself.

Yunus Emre
13TH CENTURY

A Bedouin dromedary camels guard in Petra, Jordan.

I learned much from my teachers, more from my companions,

and even more from my students.

Rabbi Yehuda ha-Nasi

2ND CENTURY C.E.

Hieroglyphics inside the temple of Pharaoh Ramses III in Luxor, Egypt.

The science of the breath is a subtle one. My friend, it is difficult enough for you to be mindful of the breaths of your body, which punctuate your life. So what can we say about the breaths of the soul and those of the spirit!

Faouzi Skali
20TH–21ST CENTURY

A child from a village near Ta'izz, Yemen.

Your daily life is your temple and your religion.

Whenever you enter into it take with you your all.

Kahlil Gibran
20TH CENTURY

A Tajik shepherd leads his flock near the 15,397-foot-high (4,693-m) Khunjerab Pass between China and Pakistan.

You may strive to be like them, but seek not to make them like you.

Kahlil Gibran
20TH CENTURY

Twin babies in a yurt in the valleys of the High Altai, Mongolia.

I don't even ask myself whether the Church itself sees me as a believer:

for me, a believer is simply someone who has faith in certain values.

And these I would reduce to a single one: human dignity.

The rest is merely hope or myth.

Amin Maalouf
20TH–21ST CENTURY

In the port of Agadir, Morocco.
OVERLEAF: An old man waits for alms from worshippers outside a mosque in the old city of Sanaa, Yemen.

August 26

None of you is a believer until he wants for

his brother what he wants for himself.

Hadith

Why was there only one Adam?

It was in order to preserve peace between people; indeed, this way

nobody can say to his neighbor: "My ancestor was greater than yours."

The Talmud

Located on the Mediterranean coast, Sabratha in Libya experienced its golden age during the first centuries of Roman rule.

Holiness begins in recognizing the face of the other.

Marc-Alain Ouaknin
20TH–21ST CENTURY

Close-up of the veiled Lebanese writer Alma Fakhre Mecattaf.

Rather rise together with the giver on his gifts as on wings.

Kahlil Gibran
20TH CENTURY

A Bactrian camel in the Hunza Valley of the Himalayas, in Pakistan.

Humanity, while it is also multiple, is primarily one.

Amin Maalouf
20TH–21ST CENTURY

A ceramic dome at the Madrasa-ye Chahar Bagh, an Islamic school in Isfahan, Iran.

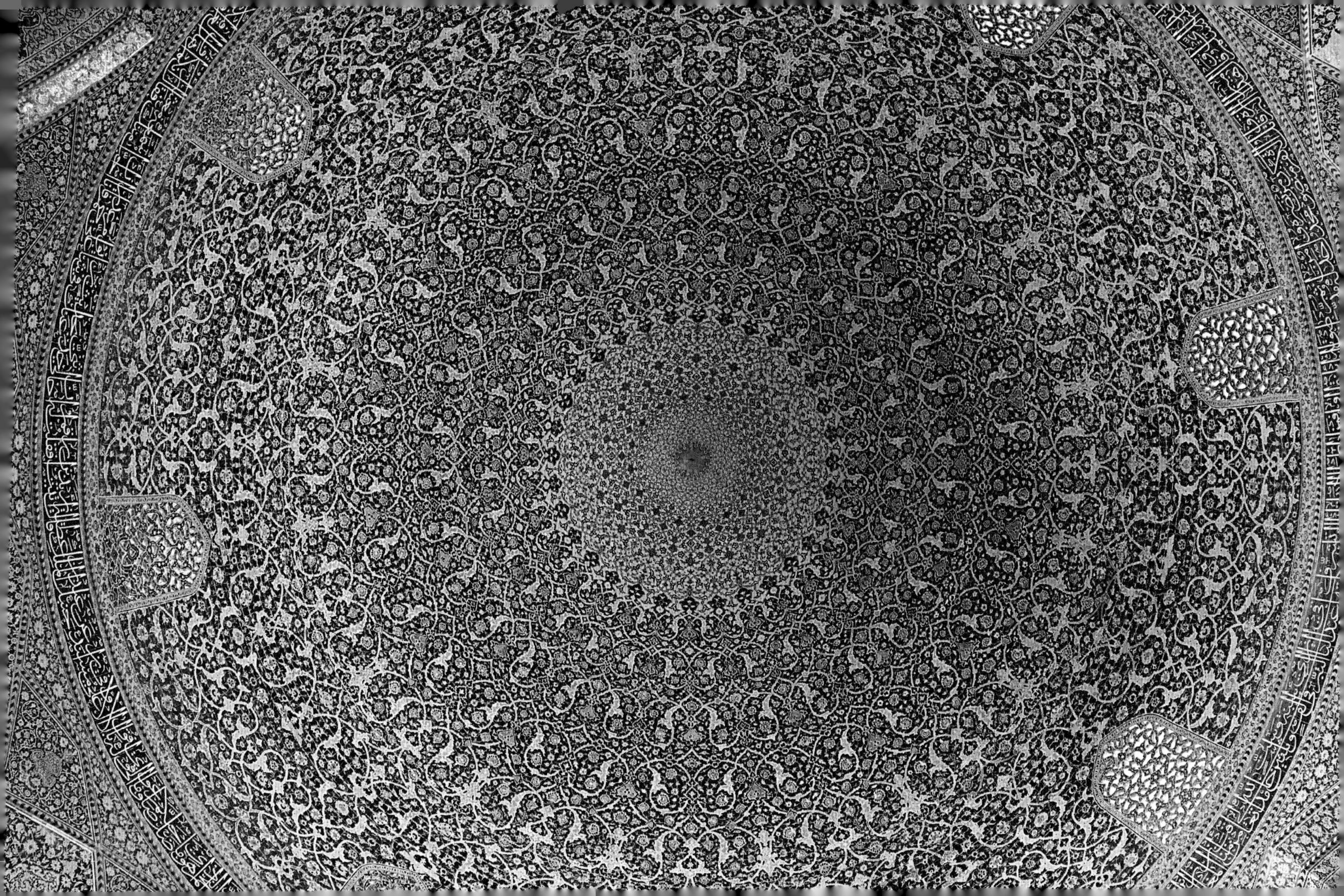

The Prophet taught us something simple but deeply important: you must take care of your neighbors.

Philippe Yacine Demaison
20TH–21ST CENTURY

In the old city of Ibb, Yemen.

If you respect someone and respect his history
it's because you believe he belongs to the same human race as you do,
not to some inferior version.

Amin Maalouf
20TH–21ST CENTURY

'Aziza Bashir Jum'a, a fifty-year-old Nubian woman, on the banks of the Nile in Egypt.
OVERLEAF: Sand dunes in the Fezzan desert south of Ghat, Libya.

September 2

The Truth you are seeking, my friend, is always beyond yourself.

Faouzi Skali
20TH–21ST CENTURY

Who is there in this world that sinned not, say—
He who sinned not, how did he live his day?
If evil I do, evil You repay,
What difference is there then between us, pray?

Omar Khayyám
11TH–12TH CENTURY

Dromedaries in the southern Sahara in Chad.

The beginning of divine wisdom is the calm born of greatness of soul

and the patience to tolerate human weakness.

Saint Isaac the Syrian
7TH CENTURY

A young Toubou shepherd in the Ennedi Mountains of Chad.

You are the way and the wayfarers.
And when one of you falls down he falls for those behind him,
a caution against the stumbling stone.
Ay, and he falls for those ahead of him,
who though faster and surer of foot,
yet removed not the stumbling stone.

Kahlil Gibran
20TH CENTURY

Riding a donkey down to the well below a village on the Atlantic coast of Morocco.

When you see your neighbor do wrong, do not incriminate him.
Rather think: "What excuse would I have conceived to exonerate myself
if I were in his place?" Apply the same excuse to your neighbor,
and do your best to exonerate him.

Rabbi Menachem Mendel of Kotsk
19TH CENTURY

Early in the morning, fishermen sell their goods on the docks of the port of Essaouira, Morocco.

Why do you look at the speck of sawdust in your brother's eye and pay

no attention to the plank in your own eye?

Saint Matthew
(MATT. 7:3)

The Uighur city of Kashgar boasts the largest market in Central Asia, a destination for traders from Kazakhstan, Tajikistan, Kyrgyzstan, Afghanistan, Pakistan, and India.

Myself when young did eagerly frequent

Doctor and Saint, and heard great argument

About it and about: but evermore

Came out by the same door as in I went.

Omar Khayyám
11TH–12TH CENTURY

In the Hunza Valley of Pakistan, most Hunzakuts are Ismaili, followers of a moderate branch of Islam whose spiritual leader is the Aga Khan.
OVERLEAF: Friends strike a deal on the banks of the Nile, Egypt.

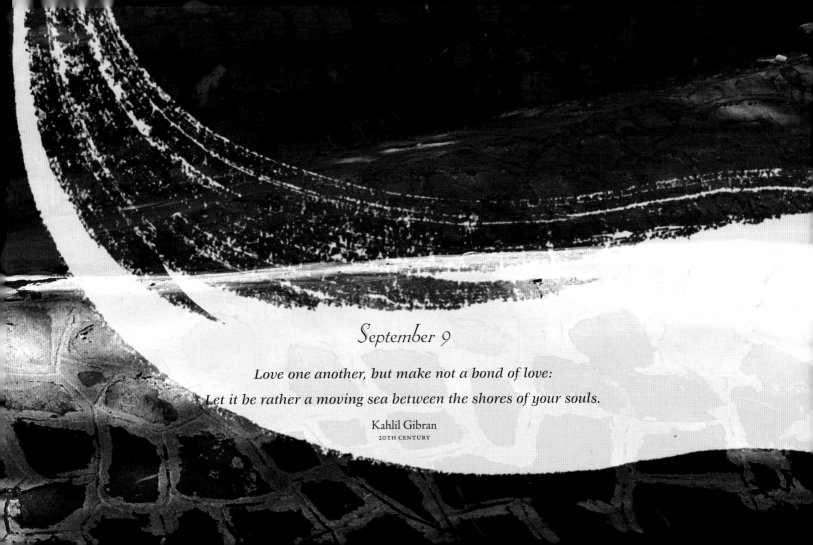

September 9

Love one another, but make not a bond of love:

Let it be rather a moving sea between the shores of your souls.

Kahlil Gibran
20TH CENTURY

It is a day neither hot nor cold,

Clouds help the dry flowers unfold

Canary with his song to the flower told

Drink while you can, yourself don't scold.

Omar Khayyám
11TH–12TH CENTURY

A felucca on the Nile in Aswan, Egypt.

The law is not the truth! Not the only truth!

The truth is plural because society is also plural.

Marc-Alain Ouaknin
20TH–21ST CENTURY

A pastoral scene in the Ta'izz region of Yemen.

He who honors you, honors Me. He who treats you with spite treats himself with spite. He who humiliates you humiliates himself.

Ibn ʿArabi
12TH–13TH CENTURY

Fishing boats in Agadir, Morocco.

Eternity is the mirror of the temporal, the temporal the mirror of pre-eternity—in this mirror those two are twisted together tresses.

Rumi
13TH CENTURY

Tahir al-Hawayji, the guardian of a traditional house in Yemen used in Pier Paolo Pasolini's film *Arabian Nights*.

That which is hateful to you, do not do to your neighbor.

This is the entire Torah; the rest is commentary. Go and learn.

Hillel the Elder
IST CENTURY B.C.E—IST CENTURY C.E.

A bust attributed to King Shebitku, son of the famous Piankhi of the Kushite Dynasty in Egypt.

If a drop of water is removed from the ocean,

eventually it will return to it.

Ahmad Muhammad Rami
20TH CENTURY

Lake Gabraoun in the oasis of Wadi al-Ajal in the Libyan Sahara.
OVERLEAF: A young fisherman in the port of Al Hudaydah, Yemen, on the Red Sea.

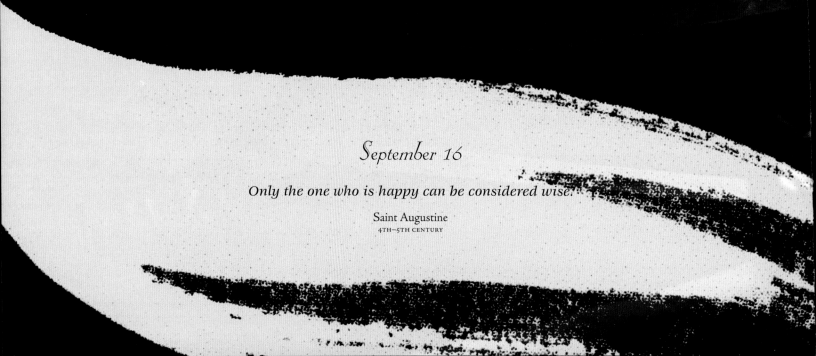

September 16

Only the one who is happy can be considered wise.

Saint Augustine
4TH–5TH CENTURY

Scorn no man and disdain no thing,
for there is no man who does not have his time
and no thing that does not find its place.

Ben Azzai
2ND CENTURY C.E.

After enjoying a meal of fresh fish, a kitten sleeps on a fisherman's net in the port of Agadir, Morocco.

Neither on a world scale nor within any society
should anybody feel so scorned, depreciated, mocked, or demonized
that in order to be able to live among his fellow-citizens
he is forced to conceal or be ashamed of his religion, color, language,
name, or any other ingredient of his identity.

Amin Maalouf
20TH–21ST CENTURY

A young woman at work in a weaving workshop in Zabid, Yemen.

Through his words, the Other is the one who questions me, wakes me up, forbids me to be old.

Marc-Alain Ouaknin
20TH–21ST CENTURY

At the Sunday market in Ta'izz, Yemen.

All things shall melt and turn into songs when spring comes.

Kahlil Gibran
20TH CENTURY

Along the road connecting Kashgar to Tashkorgan, between China, Afghanistan, and Pakistan.

The root is not the branch;

the root is one thing and the branch another.

They are not fundamentally different in the way two opposites are;

they simply do not have the same appearance.

Abu Hayyan al-Tawhidi
10TH–11TH CENTURY

The Jardin Majorelle, a garden of plants from the five continents, in Marrakech, Morocco.

Which of you would be a reed, dumb and silent,

when all else sings together in unison?

Kahlil Gibran
20TH CENTURY

On the shores of the Red Sea, fishing boats are repaired in the port of Al Hudaydah, Yemen.

September 23

I am a candle lit
by another candle.

Rabbi Akiva
1ST–2ND CENTURY C.E.

Easter mass at the Church of the Holy
Sepulchre in Jerusalem's Old City.

The image of the morning sun in a dewdrop is not less than the sun.

The reflection of life in your soul is not less than life.

Kahlil Gibran
20TH CENTURY

Ten-year-old Amman in Ghadames, Libya.

When the storm comes, and the mighty wind shakes the forest, and thunder and lightning proclaim the majesty of the sky—then let your heart say in awe, "God moves in passion."

Kahlil Gibran
20TH CENTURY

In the Haraz mountains, Ben Riyan is a mountain village typical of Yemen.

The Other's words must lead us to new evidence of unpredictable points of view by dismantling the idolatrous, prejudiced evidence of our own points of view.

Marc-Alain Ouaknin
20TH–21ST CENTURY

Muhammad Nasar, a twenty-year-old fisherman in Al Hudaydah on the Yemeni coast.

As single leaf turns yellow

but with the silent knowledge of the whole tree,

So the wrong-doer cannot do wrong without the hidden will of you all.

Kahlil Gibran
20TH CENTURY

Fishing boats in the port of Essaouira, Morocco, on the Atlantic coast.

For the length of its several thousand pages, the Talmud is a defense of the face, a plea for the recognition of the dignity of the other person in his or her particularity and infinite difference.

Marc-Alain Ouaknin
20TH–21ST CENTURY

Gaotah, a sixteen-year-old Tuareg girl at an annual celebration in Ghadames, Libya.

In short, what is purity? It is the heart's mercy for all of nature. . . .
And what is the heart's mercy? It is a flame that sets the heart ablaze
for the whole of creation: human beings, birds, quadrupeds, demons,
everything that exists.
When he thinks of them, when he looks at them, a person feels his eyes
fill with tears because of the intense compassion wringing his heart.
His heart softens and becomes incapable of tolerating, hearing, or
seeing a living creature endure the slightest wrong or affliction.

Saint Isaac the Syrian
7TH CENTURY

In the adobe city of Shibam in Hadramaut, Yemen.
OVERLEAF: Al-Muthmar al-Sufli, a mountain village in the Haraz mountains of Yemen.

September 30

My mercy encompasses all things.

The Qur'an
(7.156)

What is the end, wise man, of this journey? Is there other knowledge that the human heart could embrace? Is there a safe harbor in this unceasing change of people and things? An immutable truth?

Faouzi Skali

20TH–21ST CENTURY

A caravan near Lake Gabraoun in the Saharan region of Awbari in Libya.

The Other is the one who allows me to capitalize the word Childhood,

understood as an awakening into the heart of the One,

from awakening to division.

Marc-Alain Ouaknin
20TH–21ST CENTURY

Ten-year-old Bayan on his way to school in Zabid, Yemen.

Let us temper our judgment, let us not condemn or affirm anything in haste. The reality we judge is ephemeral. Human unhappiness resides in our haste to judge. We condemn others and condemn ourselves by asserting truths that are merely temporal.

Khaled Bentounès
20TH–21ST CENTURY

The busy Uighur city of Kashgar in Central Asia.

Always look for what is good in others.

Focus your attention on the positive aspect of the other, bring it to light,

and transform the sinner into a holy person.

Rabbi Nachman of Breslov
18TH–19TH CENTURY

The Bin Yusuf Madrasa is an old Islamic university located in the heart of Marrakech's medina.

Love is an attribute of God, who has no needs—
love for anything else is a metaphor.
The beauty of the others is gold-plated:
outwardly it is light, inwardly smoke.

Ibn 'Arabi
12TH–13TH CENTURY

The dome of Isfahan's Masjid-e Imam in Iran, one of the most beautiful mosques in the world.

I do not think there can be a link between Islam and terrorism.

Terrorism is a rejection of the other's opinion,

and Islam is a religion of freedom.

A terrorist knows nothing of Islam.

Naguib Mahfouz
20TH CENTURY

On the shores of the Red Sea, an old fisherman sells the slim catch of the day in the port of Al Hudaydah, Yemen.

October 7

In their property was a portion
dedicated to the beggar and to
the disinherited.

The Qur'an
(51.19)

A palm grove in the Moroccan Atlas.

If I know my flaws, I correct them. If I know evil, I avoid it.
It is when I do not know them, or when I consider them essences,
that they are harmful.

Khaled Bentounès
20TH–21ST CENTURY

During a three-day festival in Ghadames, Libya, Berber boys study at a madrasa, the Islamic school, in the old city.

What shall I say of him who is the pursuer

playing the part of the pursued?

Kahlil Gibran
20TH CENTURY

A cereal vendor smokes a narghile while awaiting customers in Yemen.

Come, come, whoever you are,

Wanderer, idolater, worshipper of fire, come

Even though you have broken your vows a thousand times,

come, and come yet again,

Ours is not a caravan of despair.

Rumi
13TH CENTURY

A capital of Berber culture built in an oasis, Ghadames is one of the oldest cities in Libya.

You can muffle the drum, but you can not prevent

the lark from singing.

Kahlil Gibran

20TH CENTURY

The peaceful Hunza Valley in Pakistan was for centuries the fastest route by foot to Swat and Gandhara.
The access pass was so remote that only porters, with permission from the locals, could get through.

Still more often the condemned is the burden bearer

for the guiltless and unblamed.

You cannot separate the just from the unjust and

the good from the wicked;

For they stand together before the face of the sun even as the black

thread and the white are woven together.

And when the black thread breaks, the weaver shall look into the whole

cloth, and he shall examine the loom also.

Kahlil Gibran
20TH CENTURY

Behind the Church of the Holy Sepulchre in Jerusalem's Old City, a Palestinian worker gathers a cross carried by an Easter pilgrim on the Way of the Cross.

We seek one another in our aloneness, and we walk the road when we have no hearth to sit beside.

Kahlil Gibran
20TH CENTURY

In Essaouira, Morocco, a solitary worshipper following prayers marking the end of Ramadan.
OVERLEAF: A young Toubou shepherd in the Ennedi Massif of Chad.

October 14

Man is God in slow arising;
And betwixt his joy and his pain
Lies our sleeping, and the dreaming thereof.

Kahlil Gibran
20TH CENTURY

You work that you may keep pace with the earth

and the soul of the earth.

Kahlil Gibran
20TH CENTURY

A well in the oasis of Ghadames, Libya.

Do not quarrel, for you will be weak and your power will depart.

The Qur'an
(8.46)

Used to store the grain, oil jars, and farm implements of local families, the fortified granaries of
Qasr al-Hajj, in Libya, include 114 vaulted cells, one for each chapter of the Qur'an.

As I have loved you, so you must love one another.

Saint John
(JOHN 13:34)

Byzantine frescoes and mosaics in the Church of the Holy Savior in Chora (Kariye Müzesi) in Istanbul, Turkey.

My friend, stop searching
For the why and the how
Stop spinning the wheel of your soul.
Right where you stand
At this moment
Everything is given you
In the utmost perfection.
Accept this gift
Squeeze the juice of the passing moment.

Faouzi Skali
20TH–21ST CENTURY

A Tuareg boy at an annual festival in Ghadames, Libya.

The cornerstone of the temple is not higher than the lowest stone in its foundation.

Kahlil Gibran
20TH CENTURY

Bin Yusuf Madrasa in the medina of Marrakech.

Humility will consist in recognizing that any being in the universe

can teach us what we ignore.

Rumi
13TH CENTURY

In the morning, the port of Essaouira on Morocco's Atlantic coast bustles with the arrival of fishermen.
OVERLEAF: The mountain village of Al-Muthmar al-Sufli in the Haraz mountains of Yemen.

October 21

Listen to the words of the passing moment:

"At this very moment of this long journey, where are you?"

Faouzi Skali
20TH–21ST CENTURY

It is told how a saint was meditating when, overflowing with love and compassion, he exclaimed, "My God, save all the disciples in my community!" A celestial voice then answered, "And what about the others? Did I not create them as well?"

Faouzi Skali
20TH–21ST CENTURY

Ceramics at the Madrasa-ye Chahar Bagh Islamic school in Isfahan, Iran.

Say: We believe in God and in that which had been revealed to us, and in that which was revealed to Abraham and Ishmael and Isaac and Jacob and the tribes, and in that which was given to Moses and Jesus, and in that which was given to the prophets from their Lord, we do not make any distinction between any of them, and to God do we submit.

The Qur'an
(2.136)

In the Church of the Holy Sepulchre in Jerusalem's Old City, a religious ceremony surrounding the Stone of Unction upon which Christ's body was prepared for burial.

Why, all the saints and sages who discussed

Of the two worlds so wisely—they are thrust

Like foolish prophets forth; their words to scorn

Are scattered, and their mouths are stopped with dust.

Omar Khayyám
11TH–12TH CENTURY

In the Saharan region of Awbari in Libya.

Though the glitter of the sun of the soul is the origin,

no man has reached that heaven without a body.

Rumi

13TH CENTURY

A girl in traditional dress at the Berber festival in Ghadames, Libya.

If you try to fit the ocean in a jug

How small will be your drinking mug?

Rumi
13TH CENTURY

Sunset over Morocco's Atlantic coast.

A society that neglects its youth looks like an old-age home. When it abandons its elderly, it looks like an orphanage. Blessed are the young who are inspired by the wisdom of the ancients! Blessed are the old who take heart in the enthusiasm of the young!

Jewish saying

A resident tells the story of Ghadames, a prehistoric city in Libya.

October 28

Truth is a mirror that fell from the hand of God and was broken. Everybody picked up a fragment and announced that he had found the whole truth.

Arab proverb

The dome of the Masjid-e Imam Mosque in Isfahan, Iran, with its impressive tile work and calligraphy.

Sometimes you have to keep quiet to be heard.

Stanislas Jerzy Lec
20TH CENTURY

Fatima, a nineteen-year-old Tuareg wearing traditional jewelry and hand paint in Ghadames, Libya.

Everyone should be able to include in what he regards as his own identity a new ingredient, one that will assume more and more importance in the course of the new century and the new millennium: the sense of belonging to the human adventure as well as his own.

Amin Maalouf
20TH–21ST CENTURY

Dunes in the Fezzan desert south of Ghat, Libya.

There isn't a country in the world today that doesn't need to ponder how to get different populations, local and immigrant, to live together. Everywhere there are tensions more or less skillfully contained; usually they show signs of getting worse.

Amin Maalouf
20TH–21ST CENTURY

Two Palestinian friends relax in the Old City of Jerusalem.

Set your eyes on your limits and you will perceive the Unlimited.

Faouzi Skali
20TH–21ST CENTURY

Built in the first century C.E. in Petra, Al Deir (the Monastery) was a funerary monument before it served as a refuge for Christians in Jordan.

The Orient and the Occident exist. But one who looks to God cannot be their prisoner. He belongs neither to one nor the other, but to both at once. These notions are not antithetical, but complementary. They help us grasp the harmony of the universe in its diversity. We must aim to understand these polarities without opposing them.

Khaled Bentounès
20TH–21ST CENTURY

During the Ottoman era, merchants selling goods from Europe or the southern Sahara gathered at the Hotel Zumit in Libya.

Whenever a society sees "the hand of the stranger" in modernity,

it tends to repulse it and try to ward it off.

Amin Maalouf
20TH–21ST CENTURY

A young woman shyly poses in a weaving workshop in Zabid, Yemen.
OVERLEAF: In the Ennedi Massif in the southern Sahara, Chad.

November 4

Consciousness does not consist of rejecting what
we consider to be evil but in curing it.

Khaled Bentounès
20TH–21ST CENTURY

Every man must bless the heavens for the bad things that befall him,

just as he blesses them for the good things he receives.

Rabbi Akiva
1ST–2ND CENTURY C.E.

On the ramparts that guarded the city and port of Essaouira on the Atlantic coast of Morocco.

Thanks to the sincere repentance of a single person,

the entire world is forgiven.

Rabbi Meir
2ND CENTURY C.E.

At prayer in the Suleiman Mosque (Süleymaniye Camii), Istanbul's largest mosque.

The social person is free to choose whether or not to wage an internal struggle (his great jihad) to refuse a system he considers harmful in favor of the path of serenity, peace, tolerance, and brotherhood, in harmony with nature and the satisfaction of his needs. This can be achieved through controlled development, technology employed for the well-being of all, and science based on ethics rather than conditioned by profit.

Khaled Bentounès
20TH–21ST CENTURY

Shepherds lead dromedaries to drink in the southern Sahara, in Chad.

Repentance is a great thing: it has the power to transform sin and is a way to get back on the right path.

Rabbi Yochanan ben Zakkai
1ST CENTURY C.E.

A dromedary camel in the desert in Chad.

Every rigid form is threatened with destruction. Every threat arouses hate and anger. To get past hate, you must go to the root of all forms in the secret place where love arises. From this place, my friend, the divine spark bursts forth.

Faouzi Skali
20TH–21ST CENTURY

A caravan near Lake Gabraoun in the Saharan region of Awbari, Libya.

Though liberty can be defended with weapons and equality with laws,

fraternity can only live and grow in people's hearts.

Khaled Bentounès
20TH–21ST CENTURY

Twelve-year-old Isalor Najja at a festival in Ghadames, Libya.
OVERLEAF: Lake Umm al-Maa in Libya's Saharan region of Awbari, the former home of the Daouada peoples.

November 11

The world is two worlds, spiritual and material.

Al-Ghazali
11TH–12TH CENTURY

Anyone who seeks God behind the proofs of logic is like a person who looks for the sun with a lamp in hand.

Arab proverb

On the grounds of the Coptic monastery of Saint Anthony in Egypt.

A person must always consider oneself half guilty and half innocent.

The Talmud
(KIDDUSHIN 40B)

A Nubian girl, twelve-year-old Sofia Gamal, lives with her family on the banks of the Nile in Egypt.

When you pray you rise to meet in the air those who are praying at that very hour, and whom, save in prayer, you may not meet.

Kahlil Gibran
20TH CENTURY

Praying at the Western Wall, revered as the last vestige of the Second Temple, the most sacred site in Judaism.

What are the signs of God?

The Qur'an?

Prophecy?

Creation?

Humanity?

Which one determines our faith?

Khaled Bentounès
20TH–21ST CENTURY

Bivouac on the shores of Lake Gabraoun in Awbari, Libya.

That word with which you can unlock every treasure in the world—

say it to me.

Say it to the birds, to the trees, and to the people. Repeat it to everyone:

Love is a gift, not a flaw.

Mursi Jamil 'Aziz
20TH CENTURY

A girl in traditional costume in Ghadames, Libya.

I am neither Christian, Jew, Parsi, nor Moslem. I am neither of the East nor of the West, nor of the land nor of the sea. . . . I have put aside duality, I have seen that the two worlds are one; I seek the One, I know the One, I see the One, I invoke the One. He is the First, He is the Last, He is the Outward, He is the Inward.

Rumi
13TH CENTURY

Inaugurated in 537, Istanbul's Saint Sophia was the world's largest Christian edifice until the basilica was turned into a mosque in 1453. It eventually became a museum.
OVERLEAF: On the pilgrimage route to the grotto, in Egypt, where Saint Anthony, the first Christian monk, lived as a hermit until his death in 356 C.E.

November 18

Let us not commit the fundamental error of saying or believing that

Christianity belongs to Jesus, Judaism to Moses,

and Islam to Muhammad.

Khaled Bentounès
20TH–21ST CENTURY

In the sweetness of your friendship let there be laughter,
and sharing of pleasures. For in the dew of little things
the heart finds its morning and is refreshed.

Kahlil Gibran
20TH CENTURY

An elderly Kazakh couple in the High Altai of Mongolia.

"Who would you like to have for a friend?"

"The one who catches me when I trip, puts me back on the right path if

I stray, guides me if I get lost, does not grow weary, and,

come what may, accepts me as I am."

Abu Hayyan al-Tawhidi
10TH–11TH CENTURY

Inside the Temple of Isis in Egypt.

A caress is not something you learn but an experience, an encounter.

A caress is not knowing a person but respecting that person.

A caress is neither power nor violence but tenderness.

Marc-Alain Ouaknin
20TH–21ST CENTURY

Three friends at the annual Berber festival in Ghadames, Libya.

*The love of God and of humanity is measured by their permanence,
by the strength they have to persist despite the crises and upheavals of
daily life: day and night, day and night . . .*

Rabbi Yochanan ben Zakkai
1ST CENTURY C.E.

A sandstorm in the Libyan Sahara.

A farmer taught me the real meaning of love of humanity: to love your neighbor is to feel his needs and to endure his suffering.

Rabbi Moshe Leyb of Sassov
18TH–19TH CENTURY

Twenty-year-old Yusuf at the market in Beit al-Faqih, Yemen.

The Nile flows . . . the Nile sprawls,
each wave chasing the last, trying to catch it,
to embrace it and curse the long wait.
The breeze brought them closer,
each embracing the other after a long absence.
And happiness arrived for the lovers;
each wave regained its companion.

Ahmad Muhammad Rami, sung by Umm Kulthum
20TH CENTURY

Feluccas transporting tourists on the Nile in Aswan, Egypt.
OVERLEAF: The port of Essaouira in Morocco is famous for the graceful seagulls that dance in the wind above its docks.

November 25

Sky, revolve not without me;
moon, shine not without me;
earth travel not without me;
and time, go not without me.

Rumi
13TH CENTURY

In one's early years one learns to speak, and in old age one learns to

keep quiet, and such is a person's great fault: that he learns to speak

before knowing how to keep quiet.

Rabbi Nachman of Breslov
18TH–19TH CENTURY

In the Old City of Jerusalem, a school trip to the Dome of the Rock, the third holiest site in Islam.

It would be disastrous if the current globalization were to be a one-way process, with "universal transmitters" on one side and "receivers" on the other, with the "norm" set against the "exceptions"; with on the one hand those who think they have nothing to learn from the rest of the world, and on the other those who believe that the rest of the world will never listen to them.

Amin Maalouf
20TH–21ST CENTURY

Built in 1461 in old Istanbul, the Grand Bazaar was the biggest covered market in the world for centuries.

*Improving the quality of life of the poor is,
or should be, the essence of development.*

Muhammad Yunus
20TH–21ST CENTURY

On the shores of the Red Sea in the port of Al Hudaydah, Yemen.

The ever-increasing speed of globalization undoubtedly reinforces, by way of reaction, people's need for identity. And because of the existential anguish that accompanies such sudden changes, it also strengthens their need for spirituality. But only religious allegiance meets, or at least seeks to meet, both these needs.

Amin Maalouf
20TH–21ST CENTURY

The Harbor of Agadir, on the Atlantic coast of Morocco.

Sometimes the Sun of His attributes

shines on the night of your existence

And sometimes He withdraws from you

Leaving you to your own confines.

Daylight does not come from you or go toward you

But it is reflected on you.

Faouzi Skali

20TH–21ST CENTURY

A man rests besides the exit of a mosque in the old city of Sanaa, Yemen.

My freedom doesn't end where another's commences; it begins and is realized where another's begins and is realized.

Marc-Alain Ouaknin
20TH–21ST CENTURY

Women cheer on the camel driver in a race during a festival in Ghat, Libya.

The law that delivered you into my hand shall deliver me into a mightier hand.

Kahlil Gibran
20TH CENTURY

At dawn, the catch from shark fishing is sold in the port of Al Hudaydah, Yemen.

December 3

The hero is he who smashes idols, and the idol of every man is his ego.

Ibn 'Arabi
12TH–13TH CENTURY

A student wearing the traditional Moroccan djellaba in Marrakech's Bin Yusuf Madrasa, the largest Islamic college in Morocco.

My friend, what you know of Reality is like the foam on the ocean waves. But the ocean of Being is without bottom or shore. Through its power, creatures continually emerge from their nothingness. Through its renewed gift, they survive in the foam for days. Until the day His will calls them back.

Faouzi Skali
20TH–21ST CENTURY

A fisherman on the Atlantic coast of Morocco.

What God said to the rose, that made its beauty bloom,

He has said to my heart and made it one hundred times more beautiful.

Rumi

13TH CENTURY

Eight-year-old Fatima in the village of Al-Hajjara in the Haraz mountains of Yemen.

Are the heavens richer for having brought me into this world?

Will my departure render their majesty even greater?

No one could ever tell me why

I came, or why I must leave this world.

Omar Khayyám
11TH–12TH CENTURY

A view from afar of dromedaries in the southern Sahara of Chad.

The truth of your being, my friend, is only a fragment of the infinite Truth. Whoever opens himself to the truth of his being also perceives the Truth of the universe. The drop of water rediscovers the ocean and the wave the sea.

Faouzi Skali
20TH–21ST CENTURY

The fishing port of Essaouira on the Moroccan Atlantic coast has inspired numerous artists with its beauty and tranquility.

It is the snowflake in you running down to the sea.

Kahlil Gibran
20TH CENTURY

A young Berber girl in traditional dress in Ghadames, Libya.

Wherever you are and in every circumstance,
try always to be a lover, and a passionate lover.

Rumi
13TH CENTURY

Tiles at the entrance to the Isfahan bazaar, one of the most authentic in Iran.
OVERLEAF: The Saharan region of Awbari, in the Wadi al-Ajal of Libya.

December 10

*The vision of his essence does not take place except when what has
never been disappears, and what has never ceased to be remains.*

Ibn ʿArabi
12TH–13TH CENTURY

The Path is but one step. Taking one step out of one's self to get to God.

Rumi
13TH CENTURY

A fisherman in Al Hudaydah on the Red Sea coast in Yemen.

*We think the world today is boundless, vaster than ever before. In fact,
it is poorer. A world that does not admit the presence of a God is a
world that does not admit the presence of humanity.*

Marc-Alain Ouaknin
20TH–21ST CENTURY

In Isfahan's Masjid-i Jami (Friday Mosque) in Iran.

When I want to understand what is happening today or try to decide what will happen tomorrow, I look back.

Omar Khayyám
11TH–12TH CENTURY

A girl at the festivities in Ghadames, Libya.

Fifteen billion years are but a breath in the divine order.

Khaled Bentounès
20TH–21ST CENTURY

The extreme heat in the Libyan desert accounts for this tempestuous sunset.

Thy name is on my lips

Thy image is in my eyes

Thy memory is in my heart

To whom shall I write?

Rumi
13TH CENTURY

At the annual festival in Ghadames, Libya.

The first glance unveils to the future the secrets of Eternity.

Kahlil Gibran
20TH CENTURY

A woman in the medina of Tripoli, Libya, chooses a wedding veil.
OVERLEAF: Feluccas on the Nile in Aswan, Egypt.

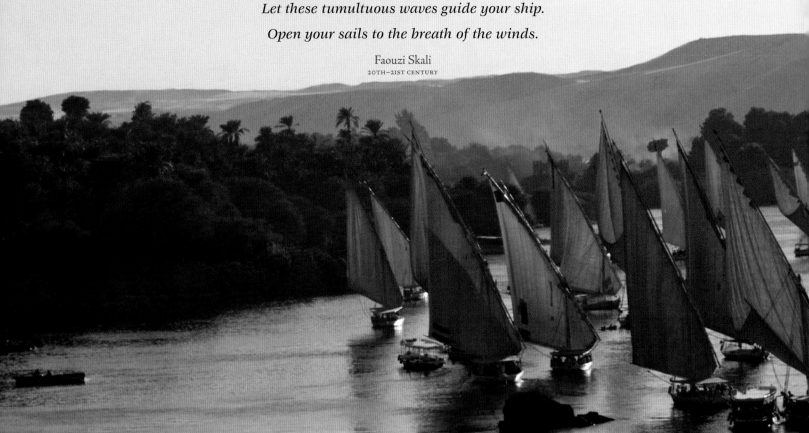

December 17

My friend, let the Truth submerge your inner moorings.

Let these tumultuous waves guide your ship.

Open your sails to the breath of the winds.

Faouzi Skali
20TH–21ST CENTURY

Where there is no truth there is no peace.

Rabbi Nachman of Breslov
18TH–19TH CENTURY

These completely veiled Hadramaut women in rural Yemen wear the typical conical straw hat.

I offer you the most beautiful of gifts:

the word "love," with which you will possess the world and all it

contains.

Mursi Jamil'Aziz
20TH CENTURY

Alma Fakhre Mecattaf, a Lebanese feminist writer.

Whoever brought me here will have to take me home.

Rumi
13TH CENTURY

The Dadès Valley, one of the most beautiful in southern Morocco.

The only one who knows peace, my friend, is the one whose heart
is free of hate. But hate has taken up residence in the hearts of men
because it defines existence.

Faouzi Skali
20TH–21ST CENTURY

Father Luc Ambabul, a Coptic monk, in the monastery of Saint Paul of Thebes in Egypt.

What is the face of God? This is the one who "faces" you: your brother, all of humanity, revolving around a single center. Through this physical and metaphysical reality, humanity takes on its full meaning.

Khaled Bentounès
20TH–21ST CENTURY

In a Kazakh yurt in Mongolia, in the High Altai mountains.

The one who has succeeded in establishing the reign of peace within himself is capable of establishing peace throughout the world.

Rabbi Simcha Bunim of Pshiskha
18TH–19TH CENTURY

A watermelon vendor near the Abakh Khoja Mausoleum in Kashgar, the Uighur city in central Asia.
OVERLEAF: Dromedaries approach a watering hole in the Ennedi Mountains in the southern Sahara region of Chad.

December 24

The sea of consciousness from which all minds derive—that is the goal of all finite minds.

Rumi
13TH CENTURY

God is beautiful and loves beauty.

Hadith

Six year old Ashar, whose Berber family lives in Ghadames, Libya.

I am a surprising thing
For the one who contemplates me.
I am the lover and the beloved.
There is no duality here.

Muhammad al-Harraq
18TH–19TH CENTURY

The lush mountains of Kyrgyzstan in the heart of Central Asia.

You are the soul of the soul of the universe, and your name is Love.

Rumi
13TH CENTURY

Colorful tile decorates the walls of Isfahan's Masjid-e Imam in Iran.

You are my life, whose dawn rises with your light.

Ahmad Shafiq Kamal
20TH CENTURY

Eight-year-old Harimna Jakih in festival attire in Ghadames, Libya.

Love calls:

Everything, at every moment.

We are leaving for the heavens.

Will you accompany us?

Rumi
13TH CENTURY

The fishing port of Essaouira on the coast of Morocco.

The essential is beyond words. It is in those lived realities, those states of being and consciousness, those inner openings of which words are only distant reflections, traces of a journey. Traces of light.

Faouzi Skali
20TH–21ST CENTURY

Reflections of fishing boats in the port of Al Hudaydah on the Red Sea coast of Yemen.
OVERLEAF: In every prayer, one humbly addresses the Creator, singing his praises and imploring his forgiveness and help.

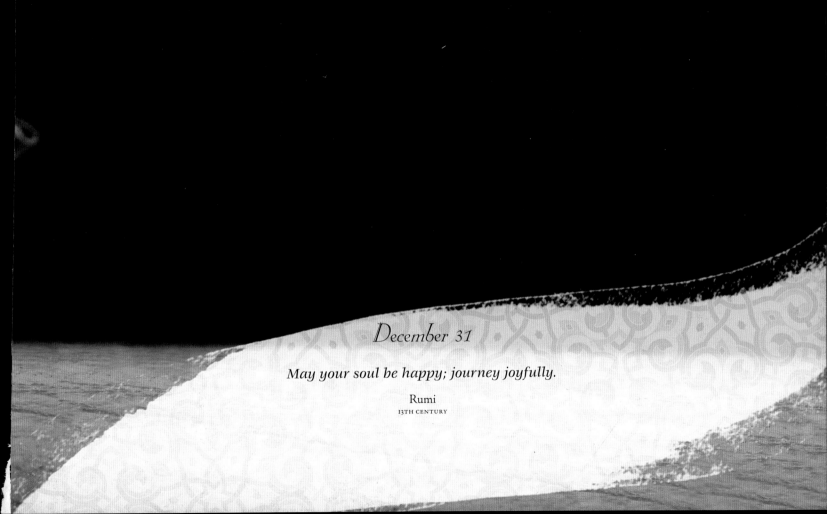

December 31

May your soul be happy; journey joyfully.

Rumi
13TH CENTURY

Biographies

One of the founders of the rabbinic tradition, **Rabbi Akiva ben Yosef,** known as **Rabbi Akiva** (c. 50 c.e.–135 c.e.), is renowned for his major role in codifying and compiling the Mishnah, the written version of the Oral Law that was created in the Holy Land during the first and second centuries c.e. Originally a poor shepherd, he began the formal study of Jewish sacred texts at forty and became a great scholar and teacher; Rabbi Meir, Shimon bar Yochai, and Yose ben Halafta were among his students. A supporter of the Bar Kokhba rebellion against Rome (132–135 c.e.), Rabbi Akiva defied the Roman ban on teaching Jewish Scripture and belief. He was imprisoned and died as a martyr.

Ibn 'Arabi (1165–1240) was born in Murcia in Muslim Spain, and died in Damascus, Syria. A Muslim philosopher and mystic who aimed to bring together the traditional and esoteric currents of Islam, he is considered the greatest Sufi master and his vast body of work the towering achievement of Sufism. Before Ibn 'Arabi, Sufism was considered a mystical belief; he contributed its intellectual dimension and had a profound influence on future generations of thinkers.

Farid al-Din 'Attar, known as **'Attar** (12th–13th century), is one of the most renowned Persian Sufi poets and mystics. Sufism is a mystical form of Islam that seeks union with God through personal experience. Sufi poetry, such as 'Attar's *Conference of the Birds,* is a vehicle for the expression of Sufi meditations and teachings. An indefatigable traveler, he met Rumi and several other great Sufi mystics. His writings include an account of the sayings and experiences of seventy-two Sufi saints. It is said that he wrote a hundred thousand verses.

Born in Thagaste in present-day Algeria, **Saint Augustine** (354–430 c.e.) was the Catholic bishop of Hippo and a major philosopher and theologian who wrote in Rome during late antiquity and was later canonized as a saint. He is one of the principal Fathers of the Latin Church. Aside from Saint Paul, he is considered the most important figure in the development of Christianity and the only Church father whose writings have given rise to a system of thought—Augustinism. Among his important writings are the autobiographical *Confessions* (c. 398), presenting concepts of time and memory that have had an impact on modern thought and literature, and *The City of God* (413–26).

Israel ben Eliezer, the **Baal Shem Tov**, or Master of the Good Name (1698–1760), is the founder of Hasidism, a mystical pietist movement that had a major impact on Jewish life and religious practice, especially during the eighteenth and nineteenth centuries in Eastern Europe. Born in a village in Podolia, now in the Ukraine, the Baal Shem Tov spent time in the Carpathian mountains doing manual labor and communing with nature. He later became a teacher and a purported miracle worker. He did not leave any writings, but his oral teachings were spread through tales, aphorisms, and sermons of students who became acclaimed Hasidic masters; the earliest collection was published in1814 as *Shivhei ha-Besht* (In Praise of the Baal Shem Tov).

Tahar Ben Jelloun (b. 1944) is a Moroccan writer and poet born in Fez. After receiving doctorates in philosophy and in social psychiatry, he wrote *L'Enfant de sable* (Child of Sand), the novel that brought him fame and prestigious prizes. He has also written several nonfiction works on important cultural topics, including *Le Racisme expliqué à ma fille* (Racism Explained to My Daughter). His work has been translated into many languages.

Shaykh Khaled Bentounès (b. 1949) is the Algerian heir of a long line of Sufi masters that traces its descent from the Prophet Muhammad. He seeks to share a culture of peace and brotherhood aimed at bringing together the efforts of diverse people. A man of both meditation and action, he has committed himself to cultural and social initiatives in both France and Algeria.

The Bible is a collection of sacred texts on which the Jewish and Christian religions base their theology and spirituality. Christians study the Old Testament, as they call the Hebrew Bible, and the New Testament, which centers on the life and teachings of Jesus Christ; it contains the Gospels, Epistles, Acts, and Revelations. The Hebrew Bible, or Tanach, consists of the Five Books of Moses, known as the Torah; the historical and prophetic books, such as Jeremiah and Isaiah; and the Writings, such as Psalms and Proverbs.

Philippe Yacine Demaison (20th century), who is engaged in improving the situation of young people in the suburbs of Paris, participated in founding Scouts de France, the French Scouts. He has collaborated on various books, including *L'Islam dans la cité* (Islam in the Housing Projects) and *Dialogue avec les jeunes musulmans français* (Dialogue with Young French Muslims).

Rabbi Elisha ben Abuyah (1st century C.E.), born in Jerusalem and a contemporary of Rabbi Akiva, was one of the *tannaim*, rabbinic sages who compiled the Mishnah during the first and second centuries C.E. He is the most famous Jewish apostate of that era. A brilliant student, he is referred to in the Talmud as *acher*—the Other, one who broke with Jewish tradition and authorities. In the play *Elisha ben Abuyah* Elisha is portrayed actor Jacob Adler as an ethical man who is both a heretic and a Jew.

Yunus Emre (13th–14th century) is a Turkish Sufi poet who was a contemporary of important Sufi literary figures such as Rumi. Influenced by Anatolian folk poetry, he has enriched Turkish culture with his ideas and approach to life. By means of his poetry, he spread his love of God and a message of peace for mankind.

Mursi Jamil 'Aziz (20th century) is a celebrated Egyptian poet and lyricist whose lyrics have been sung by the Egyptian Umm Kulthum and Muharram Fouad. Umm Kulthum sings about religion, love, and the Egyptian nation.

Genesis is the first book of the Torah, the Hebrew Bible, and also of the Old Testament, as the first part of the Christian Bible is known. It recounts the origins of humanity, the creation of the world, and the lives of the Hebrew patriarchs.

Abu Hamid Muhammad bin Muhammad al-Tusi al-Ghazali, also known as **al-Ghazali** (1058–1111), is an emblematic figure of Islam; one of the greatest Islamic philosophers, a theologian, mystic, and scholar of Sufism. Al-Ghazali was born in Khorasan, then Persia. After following an advanced course of philosophical study at the university in Baghdad, he became a scholar, teacher, and prolific writer, publishing more than seventy books. His writings combine ideas from philosophy and theology; al-Ghazali also discussed science and psychology, and even advanced a theory of "atomic" particles.

Kahlil Gibran (1883–1931) is one of the great poets, artists, and philosophers of the Middle East. Born in northern Lebanon to a poor Christian Maronite family, he studied at Beirut's Sagesse High School, where he took courses in Arabic and French, religion and ethics. Enamored with painting, he moved to Paris, where he studied with Rodin, and encountered symbolist artists such as Debussy. He eventually settled in New York, where he would remain for the rest of his life. He is widely known for his book *The Prophet* (1926), a classic of spirituality and an international best-seller that was especially popular in the United States during the 1960s. A politically committed intellectual, Gibran headed a political and literary organization dedicated to supporting the countries of the Middle East.

Hadith refers to the collections of oral traditions that record the words and acts of the Prophet Muhammad; it is considered a source of the teachings of Muhammad and Islam; commentary on the Qur'an; as well as interpretations of Islamic law, ethics, history, biography, and customs. Hadith is composed of a basic narrative along with commentary. Originally oral narrative, Hadith was compiled in written form during the eighth and ninth centuries (C.E.).

Hafiz (1325–1389) is one of the most celebrated Persian lyric poets and one of the best known to international readers. He was born and died in Shiraz and remains hugely popular in Iran, where most people can recite entire verses of his work; his grave is a pilgrimage site.

Rabbi Hanina ben Dosa (1st century C.E.) was one of the first-century C.E. *tannaim*, sages whose rulings and sayings are recorded in the

Mishnah. Many anecdotes refer to his humility, fervent devotion, and miracle-working powers.

Muhammad al-Harraq (1772–1845) is a distinguished Moroccan poet who was acquainted with most of the great Middle Eastern Sufis. His agile synthesis of the leading currents of thought became a major source of initiation into Sufism in North Africa. He chose to live in Mecca, at the crossroads of the various influences that shaped the Arab world.

Hillel the Elder (1st century B.C.E.–1st century C.E.) was born in Babylonia but lived in Jerusalem during the period of the Second Temple, the reigns of Herod and Augustus, and the early years of Jesus. He was a teacher of the sages who compiled the Mishnah, the foundational text of the Talmud. Although he started as a woodcutter, he became the foremost scholar and teacher of the Torah and Jewish law.

Saint Isaac the Syrian (7th century) was born in present-day Qatar and lived in the region administered by the Mesopotamian Nestorian Church. He was ordained bishop of Nineveh around 676, when he was still a young monk. He left his office to live as a hermit. The *Ascetical Homilies*, his best-known work, considers themes such as the mystery of God-Love and Christ the Savior.

Edmond Jabès (1912–1991) was born in Cairo to a Jewish family. His work is noted for its reflections on exile and Jewish identity. The winner of innumerable prizes in the arts, letters, and sciences and lecturer around the world, he facilitated the exchange of culture and memory across the Mediterranean.

Saint John (1st century) was born in the village of Bethsaida in Galilee in present-day Israel. A precursor and apostle of Jesus Christ, he is also known as John the Apostle, John the Evangelist, or John the Theologian. He wrote the fourth Gospel, which bears his name, and the Book of Revelations, also known as the Apocalypse of John.

Ahmad Shafiq Kamal (20th century) is an Egyptian poet. He wrote the lyrics to many songs for Uum Kulthum, the Egyptian diva known as "The Star" and a prominent symbol of Egyptian national unity.

Omar Khayyám (11th–12th century) was a Persian mathematician, astronomer, and philosopher best known as the author of one of the most popular poetic texts in the world, the *Rubaiyat*; consisting of four-line quatrains, the *Rubaiyat* was translated into English by Edward Fitzgerald in the nineteenth century. Rejecting prevailing Islamic beliefs, Omar Khayyám searched for truth in science, philosophy, and the pleasures of life; he dared to doubt everything that was venerated around him.

The Qur'an, or Koran, the sacred book of Islam, is considered by Muslims to be the holy and uncreated word of God (Allah) addressed to all humanity. A collection of texts revealed to the Prophet Muhammad directly from God during the course of twenty-three years, beginning in c. 609 C.E., it continues to be memorized and transmitted from one generation to the next. It consists of 114 chapters known as sura. The Qur'an was transmitted orally by Muhammad when he was alive, and written and codified during the caliphate of Abu Bakr, the Prophet's successor; an authoritative text was completed c. 650. The Qur'an is a source of moral guidance and truth in the Muslim Faith.

Stanislas Jerzy Lec (1909–1966) was born in Lwow, then Lemberg, Galicia, which was part of the Austro-Hungarian Empire. His wealthy family was of Jewish origin, but had converted to Christianity. Lec studied law in Lwow and engaged in Socialist political activities, opposing the Communist regime in Poland, which led to censorship of his work as a writer. However, in 1957, he was permitted to publish a series of satirical poems and became famous for his brilliant aphorisms.

Born in Antioch in Asia Minor, near the border with present-day Syria, **Saint Luke** (1st century) was a converted pagan, a physician, and a faithful associate of Saint Paul. He wrote the third Gospel of the New Testament, which bears his name, and is attributed to be the author of the Acts of the Apostles. Following Paul to Rome, he aided him during the time of Paul's martyrdom.

Born to a Christian family in Beirut, Lebanon, **Amin Maalouf** (b. 1949) studied economics and sociology before becoming a journalist and traveling to more than sixty countries as a foreign correspondent. Heavily influenced by his experiences of civil war and immigration, Maalouf's writings are concerned with uprooted people facing issues of cultural, political, linguistic, and religious identity. Since 1975, he has lived in Paris.

Naguib Mahfouz (1911–2006) is the only writer in the Arabic language to receive the Nobel Prize in Literature—in 1988. Born in Cairo, he graduated from the University of Cairo in philosophy; but he became a journalist and then a civil servant, directing various cultural agencies. At the same time, he began his extraordinarily prolific career as a writer: he wrote 34 novels, volumes of short stories, as well as plays and film scripts. Many of his novels are set in the Cairo neighborhood in which he was born, el-Gamaleyya, which he vividly brings to life. His major works include the *Cairo Trilogy* (1956–57), a family saga set in Cairo from World War I to the 1950s; the allegorical *Children of Gebelawi* (1959); *Miramar* (1967), in which the author makes use of modernist narrative techniques; and a historical novel, *Akhnaten, Dweller in Truth* (1985). A humanist and defender of freedom of expression, Mahfouz examined Egyptian history and culture from antiquity to modern times as well as contemporary Egyptian society with its tensions between tradition and modernity.

Saint Matthew, also known as Matthew the Evangelist (1st century), was born in Galilee and is said to have worked as a tax collector for Herod. A follower of Jesus Christ, he was one of the twelve Apostles and known as the author of the first Gospel, which is the first book of the New Testament. The Gospel according to Matthew narrates the life and work of Jesus, as well as His death and resurrection. Presenting Jesus as fulfilling Old Testament prophecy, the Gospel is often described as directed to the Hebrews. Matthew was martyred in Ethiopia in 61 C.E.

Rabbi Meir (2nd century C.E.), a disciple of Rabbi Elisha ben Abuyah and Rabbi Akiva, is one of the *tannaim*, rabbinic sages who recorded the Oral Law and teachings of the first- and second-century C.E. rabbis in the Mishnah, a core text of the Talmud. Rabbi Meir is said to have earned his living as a scribe, but he is known in the Talmud as a legendary teacher and miracle worker. He is buried in Tiberias, Israel.

Rabbi Menachem Mendel of Kotsk (1787–1859), born in Lublin, Poland, was a charismatic leader of Polish Hasidism. A disciple of Simcha Bunim of Pshiskha, he railed against the excesses of some Hasidic dynasties and protested worldliness in all its forms. His incisive, paradoxical teachings emphasize individuality in devotion and action, and, in the tradition of Polish Hasidism, favored Torah study and learning as well as fervent prayer.

Midrash has two basic meanings. First, it is a type of rabbinic text that was especially popular from 400 through 1200 C.E.. There is no single text called the Midrash, but rather a collection of texts focused on interpreting biblical law and narrative and, to a lesser degree, other sacred works. In addition, Midrash signifies a "process" of biblical exegesis, ranging from the literal meaning; deeper explanation; comparative analysis; to the deepest layer of hidden meaning, or mystery. As text and process, Midrash fills in the gaps in biblical narrative, elaborating the basic text with reference to history, customs, law, ethics, literature, and scholarly sources.

Iraj Mirza (1874–1926), a Persian poet and member of the royal family, received an education that combined Oriental and Western learning.

Aside from his fluent Arabic and French, he spoke English and Russian. His work introduced new themes, such as social justice and the status of women, into Iranian poetry.

Muhammad (c. 570–632 C.E.; d. 11 A.H.), the central figure of Islam, is regarded as the prophet and messenger of God, or Allah. Born in Mecca, in the Arabian Peninsula, he was orphaned as a young child and later became a merchant; for many years, he spent time in spiritual retreat and meditation. According to Islamic belief, at the age of 40, during the month of Ramadan, Muhammad received the first of numerous revelations from the angel Gabriel, in Arabic, that are recorded in the *Qur'an*, or Koran, as the word of God. Three years later, he began to preach, proclaiming himself the messenger and prophet of God in the tradition of Abraham, Moses, and Jesus. Following years of conflict with opponent groups in Mecca, he migrated to Medina in 622; that journey, known as the Hegira, or *hijra*, marks the first year in the Islamic calendar (A.H., anno Hegirae). Muhammad and his followers eventually conquered their opponents in Mecca, establishing Islam in Arabia. In 632, he made his first pilgrimage to Mecca, in which the rites of the *hajj* were established; the Prophet died in Medina in 632.

Rabbi Nachman of Breslov (1772–1810) may be considered the last of the great Jewish mystics. A great-grandson of the Baal Shem Tov, the founder of Hasidism, he became the spiritual leader of the Breslov Hasidim in Ukraine. He aimed to revitalize Hasidism through inspired teaching, Torah study, and worship, as well as new forms of spiritual expression. Perhaps foremost among these forms are the complex tales that Rabbi Nachman himself created and told in Yiddish. Rabbi Nachman's disciple Nathan of Nemirov inscribed the tales, which were then published to popular acclaim, making Nachman one of the most influential voices in Hasidism.

Marc-Alain Ouaknin (b. 1957) is a philosopher and rabbi who was born in Paris. Director of the Jewish Research and Study Center in Paris and a professor of comparative literature at Bar-Ilan University in Israel, much of his scholarly work has focused on the philosophy of Emmanuel Levinas in the context of Jewish thought, the Kabbalah, and Hasidism.

Born in Istanbul, Turkey, **Orhan Pamuk** (b. 1952) originally intended to become a painter or an architect; but after studying journalism at Istanbul University, he turned to writing. His novels are set in the wealthy, modern Istanbul neighborhood in which he grew up as well as in Turkey's rich Ottoman past. Important works include *The Black Book* (1990; 1994); *My Name Is Red* (2001); *Snow* (2004); and his memoir *Istanbul: Memories and the City* (2005). His novels are acclaimed for their ability to conjure the spirit, atmosphere, and complex rhythms of Istanbul, along with the cultural alienation expressed in tensions between East and West, tradition and modernity. Pamuk's work has been translated into more than twenty languages. In 2006, Orhan Pamuk was awarded the Nobel Prize in Literature.

Saint Paul (c. 10 C.E.–c. 65 C.E.), also known as Paul the Apostle, was originally called Saul of Tarsus. At the time that the disciples of Jesus were beginning to preach Christian doctrine, Saul was a rabbi teaching Scripture in Jerusalem. Initially a persecutor of Christians, he converted to Christianity as a result of a revelation on the road to Damascus and took the name Paul. Traveling through Asia Minor, Greece, and even to Rome as an evangelist, Paul inspired numerous conversions everywhere he passed; his epistles form an important part of the New Testament. He was martyred in Rome after fifteen years of preaching.

Ahmad Muhammad Rami (1892–1981) was a polyglot Egyptian poet who translated Shakespeare's English and Omar Khayyám's Persian into Arabic. He is known as the "poet of the young" because of the many songs in Arabic he has written for young people. He is notable also for writing 137 song lyrics for the internationally renowned Egyptian singer, musician, and actress Umm Kulthum.

Driven with his family from his birthplace of Balkh, in Afghanistan, by the Mongolian invasions, **Jalal al-Din Rumi,** known as **Rumi** (1207–1273), went on to become the greatest mystic poet in the Persian language. His poems are among the most sublime examples of universal spiritual poetry, particularly the *Masnavi*, a 51,000-verse masterpiece that continues to be read and meditated. A great spiritual master known throughout the East as the *Mawlana*, the ultimate master, he is the founder of the Mawlawi Sufi order known as the Whirling Dervishes, in which dance is an integral part of religious ceremony and spiritual experience. Although his poetry and ideas are embedded in Islam, Rumi enjoyed the company of Christians and Jews as much as that of his fellow believers.

Frithjof Schuon (1907–1998) was born in Basel, Switzerland. He worked as an illustrator in Paris. Eager to learn about all religions, including Christianity and Islam, he traveled to Algeria to seek enlightenment from the great Sufi masters before founding one of the first branches of Islamic esotericism in Europe.

The Persian poet and philosopher **Mahmud Shabistari** (13th–14th century) was a Persian Sufi mystic. His major work, *The Rose Garden of the Secrets (Golchan-e raz)*, is a classic of Persian literature. He remains an acclaimed poet in Iran, where one can also visit his grave.

Rabbi Shimon bar Yochai (2nd century C.E.), known by the acronym *Rashbi*, lived in the Holy Land during the Mishnaic period from 70–200 C.E. A student of Rabbi Akiva during the Roman persecutions, according to legend he hid from authorities for several years by living in a cave. Cited frequently in the Talmud, he is acknowledged as the author of the Zohar, a major text of Jewish mysticism.

Rabbi Simcha Bunim of Pshiskha (1765–1827) was an important leader of Polish Hasidism. A disciple of Rabbi Jacob Isaac of Pshiskha (or Przysucha), known as the "Holy Jew," he worked as a pharmacist before becoming the rebbe, or charismatic leader, of the Pshiskha school. Simcha Bunim emphasized the centrality of understanding the human being, perhaps even more important than understanding God, in order to achieve spiritual awareness. His most important disciple was Rabbi Menachem Mendel of Kotsk.

Born in Fez, Morocco, **Faouzi Skali** (20th century) is a Sufi teacher, scholar, author, and cultural visionary dedicated to the pursuit of *tariqah*, the Sufi mystic path. A man of action, he launched important international conferences to promote dialogue among diverse religions and cultures, among them the internationally renowned Fez Festival of World Sacred Music, and the Institute for Intercultural and Inter-religious Dialogue in Ifrane, a network for cultural dialogue devoted to opening the door to "enlightened" Islam. His writings include *La voie ufi* (The Sufi Path) and *Le face à face des coeurs: Le Soufisme aujourd'hui* (A Dialogue of Hearts: Sufism Today).

The Talmud is the second most important Jewish text, after the Hebrew Bible, or Torah. It consists of two parts: the Mishnah, the written record of oral discussions on the Torah passed down through the generations and compiled during the first two centuries C.E.; and the Gemara, the collection of commentary and discussions on the Mishnah. The Talmud is partly a legal document, presenting rulings based on biblical interpretation; but the rabbis' discussions range across many topics, including oral traditions, legends, lives of the sages, customs, ethics, history, and biblical exegesis.

Abu Hayyan al-Tawhidi (10th–11th century) lived in Baghdad and later in Persia; he wrote in Arabic and is considered one of the handful of great masters of classical Arabic prose. A grammarian, philosopher, moralist, and mystic, he left a highly diverse body of work, of which only a few fragments have been translated. His philosophical writings explore Neoplatonic and Gnostic ideas within a literary context; he is also the author of an essay on friendship and a symposium on literature and philosophy called *Enjoyment and Conviviality*.

Saint Thomas (1st century) is one of the twelve Apostles who accompanied Jesus Christ. Revered in the Eastern Orthodox as well as Western Church, he is known as the evangelizer of the Indies for bringing Christianity to the East, including Syria and India; he died a martyr in India.

The Torah, from a Hebrew word for Law, is the fundamental text of Judaism and the basis of the Abrahamic monotheistic religions. Essentially, Torah refers to the Five Books of Moses, known as the Pentateuch. But it is often defined more broadly to include the entire Hebrew Bible as well as oral and written commentary on the Bible. Torah may also be understood to signify, even more broadly, the spiritual knowledge and teachings revealed in the sacred text.

Mahmud Bayram al-Tunisi (1893–1961) was the pioneer of modern Egyptian folkloric poetry. After 1920, he lived in exile in France and Tunisia. As lyricist, he wrote songs for the Egyptian star Umm Kulthum. His songs can still be heard on every Middle Eastern radio station in all the languages of the Arab Middle East.

Umm Kulthum (1904–1975) was born Fatima Ibrahim al-Sayyid al-Beltagui in Egypt. Noticed at an early age by a famous singer, she displayed an exceptional talent for singing, but she did not begin to perform in public until a few years later, at sixteen, appearing in small theaters dressed as a boy. Fortuitous encounters with two virtuosos, a poet and a lute player, opened the doors to the palace of Arabic theater and success. Umm Kulthum undertook major tours of the Middle East, performing in Damascus, Baghdad, Beirut, Tripoli, and other cities. She was known as the "singer of the people" for her charitable work and her generosity toward the poor. Her majestic funeral was attended by more than 5 million people.

Rabbi Yehuda ha-Nasi (135–219 C.E.), also known as Judah the Prince, was a descendant of Hillel and, through his mother, of the royal House of David. A great scholar, he was the major rabbinical authority of his generation, and renowned as the chief editor of the Mishnah, who organized the discussions of the first- and second-century rabbis into a written text composed of six treatises.

Rabbi Yochanan ben Zakkai (1st century C.E.) was a student of Hillel the Elder. The first disciple to be given the title of rabbi, he lived during the troubled times of the Jewish wars with Rome that climaxed with the destruction of the Second Temple in 70 C.E. After Jerusalem lay in ruins, he established a center of Jewish learning in Yavneh, where he and other first-century rabbis in the Council of Yavneh formulated the traditions of rabbinic Judaism that would replace priestly worship in the Temple. He is said to have also organized the biblical canon.

Muhammad Yunus (b. 1940), from Bangladesh, is a economist and entrepreneur. The winner of the Nobel Peace Prize in 2006, he is famous for having founded the first microcredit organization, the Grameen Bank. He is known as the "banker to the poor."

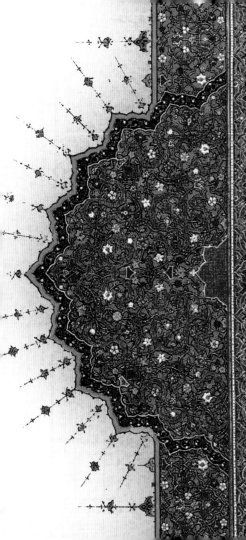

Bibliography

Addas, Claude. Ibn 'Arabi: *The Voyage of No Return*. Cambridge, U.K.: Islamic Texts Society, 2000: Sept. 12; Dec. 3 and 10. REPRODUCED BY KIND PERMISSION OF THE ISLAMIC TEXTS SOCIETY, © ISLAMIC TEXTS SOCIETY, 2000

The Bible: Apr. 3; July 1 and 4; Sept. 7; Oct. 17.

Ben Jelloun, Tahar. "Soumission à la paix." *Le Monde des religions: 20 clés pour comprendre l'islam,* hors série no. 4 (2007): July 6.

Bentounès, Khaled. *L'Homme intérieur à la lumière du Coran.* Paris: Éditions Albin Michel, 1998: Jan. 5; Feb. 25; Mar. 6 and 22; Apr. 28; May 18 and 19; June 10, 16, and 29; July 11, 14, and 22; Aug. 5 and 13; Oct. 3 and 8; Nov. 2, 4, 7, 10, 15, and 18; Dec. 14 and 22.

Buccianti, Alexandre. "Le gouvernement égyptien accélère son programme de démantèlement du secteur public." *Le Monde,* December 23, 1994): Oct. 6.

Demaison, Philippe Yacine. *L'Islam dans la cité : dialogue avec les jeunes musulmans français.* Paris: Éditions Albin Michel, 2006: Mar. 5; June 2; Aug. 31.

Deseille, Placide. *La spiritualité orthodoxe et la philocalie.* Paris: Éditions Albin Michel, 2003: Sept. 4 and 29.

Emre, Yunus. *Le petit livre des Conseils.* Translated from Turkish and edited by André Duchemin. Paris: Éditions Arfuyen, 2006: Aug. 10 and 20.

FitzGerald, Edward. *Rubáiyát of Omar Khayyám: A Critical Edition.* Edited by Christopher Decker. Charlottesville and London: University Press of Virginia, 1997.

al-Ghazali. *The Niche for Lights.* Lahore, Pakistan: Sh. M. Ashraf, 1952: Jan. 24; Feb. 7 and 15; Nov. 11.

Gibran, Kahlil. *The Earth Gods.* New York: Alfred A. Knopf, 1968.
_____. *The Eye of the Prophet.* Berkeley, CA: Frog Books, 1995.
_____. *The Garden of the Prophet.* New York: Alfred A. Knopf, 1960.
_____. *The Prophet.* New York: Knopf, 1951.
_____. *Le Sable et l'écume: Aphorismes.* Paris: Éditions Albin Michel, 1990.
Jan. 3, 10, 13, 26, and 31; Feb. 2, 4, 5, 17, 19, 23, and 28; Mar. 11, 15, 16, 20, 23, 25, 27, 29, and 31; Apr. 6, 7, 13, 17, 18, 19, 22, 24, 25, 27, and 29; May 6, 10, 12, 14, 16, 21, 23, 26, and 30; June 1, 3, 6, 9, and 28; July 19, 20, and 21; Aug. 1, 4, 11, 12, 14, 15, 17, 23, 24, and 29; Sept. 5, 9, 20, 22, 24, 25, and 27; Oct. 9, 11, 12, 13, 14, 15, and 19; Nov. 14 and 19; Dec. 2, 8, and 16.

Ibn 'Arabi. *Le chant de l'ardent désir.* Arles, France: Éditions Actes Sud, 1995.
_____. *Traité de l'amour.* Arles, France: Éditions Albin Michel, 1986. Jan. 19; Feb. 11; June 27; Sept. 12; Oct. 5.

Haddith. Apr. 8; Aug. 26; Dec. 25.

Khayyám, Omar. *Quatrains-Ballades.* Arles, France: Éditions Actes Sud, 1998.
_____. *Les quatrains d'Omar Khayyâm.* Translated and edited by Omar Ali-Shah. Paris: Éditions Albin Michel, 2005.
_____. *Ruba'iyat.* Berkeley, CA: Asian Humanities Press, 1991.
Feb. 12; Apr. 21; June 8 and 27; July 5 and 12; Sept. 3, 8, and 10; Oct. 5 and 24; Dec. 3, 6, 10, and 13.

Khemir, Nasser. *Bab 'Aziz, le prince qui contemplait son âme.* Paris: Les Films du Requin, 2006.

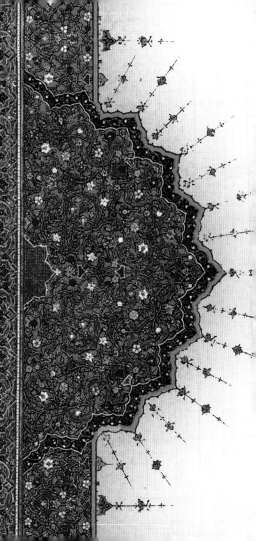

The Qur'an: May 3; Aug. 19; Sept. 30; Oct. 7, 16, and 23.

Lurçat, Pierre Itshak. *Préceptes de vie issus de la sagesse juive.* Paris: Presses du Châtelet, 2001: Jan. 2 and 11; Feb. 6 and 9; Mar. 1 and 3; Apr. 1, 4 and 23; May 24, 27, and 28; June 18, 19, and 21; July 17, 26, and 30; Aug. 3, 7, and 27; Sept. 6 and 14; Oct. 4; Nov. 23; Dec. 18.

Maalouf, Amin. *On Identity.* London: Harvill, 2000: Jan. 20; Feb. 24; Mar. 24; June 15; Aug. 25 and 30; Sept. 1 and 18; Oct. 30 and 31; Nov. 3, 27, and 29.

Mahfouz, Naguib. *Impasse des deux palais.* Paris: Éditions Jean-Claude Lattès, 1985: Jan. 12.

Malka, Victor. *Mots d'esprit de l'humour juif.* Paris: Éditions du Seuil, 2006.
_____. *Proverbes de la sagesse juive.* Paris: Éditions du Seuil, 1994.
_____. *Les sages du judaïsme, Vie et enseignements.* Paris: Éditions du Seuil, 2007.
Feb. 14; Mar. 7 and 18; Apr. 10 and 12; May 4; July 9; Aug. 2, 8, 18, and 21; Sept. 17 and 23; Oct. 27 and 29; Nov. 5, 6, 8, and 22; Dec. 23.

Mégally, Samir. *L'Egypte chantée 2, Oum Kalthoum.* Paris: Éditions Samir Mégally, 1997: Mar. 10, 12, 21, and 30; Apr. 5 and 14; May 2; June 5; Sept. 15; Nov. 16 and 24; Dec. 19 and 28.

Merton, Thomas. *La Sagesse du désert, Aphorismes des pères du désert.* Paris: Éditions Albin Michel, 2006: Feb. 18; May 22; July 15; Nov. 12.

Midal, Fabrice. *L'essentiel de la sagesse soufie.* Paris: Presses du Châtelet, 2006: Jan. 18.

Ouaknin, Marc-Alain. *Lire aux éclats. Eloge de la caresse.* Paris: Éditions du Seuil, 1994: Jan. 17, 21, and 22; May 1, 11, and 20; June 11, 12, 13, 14, 25, and 30; July 10; Aug. 28; Sept. 11, 19, 26, and 28; Oct. 2; Nov. 21; Dec. 1 and 12.

Pamuk, Orhan. Nobel Lecture at the Swedish Academy, Stockholm (December 7, 2006): May 9.

Paroles de Touaregs. Text compilation by Maguy Vautier. Paris: Éditions Albin Michel, 1997: Mar. 19.

Rumi, Jalal al-Din. *The Book of Love.* San Francisco: HarperSanFrancisco, 2003.
_____. *The Essential Rumi.* Edison, NJ: Castle Books, 1997.
_____. *The Masnavi,* vol. 2. New York: Oxford University

Press, 2007. BY PERMISSION OF OXFORD UNIVERSITY PRESS.
_____. *Mystical Poems* (second edition). Boulder, CO:
Westview Press, 1979.
Jan. 4 and 29; Feb. 1, 3, 13, 16, 21, and 22; Mar. 4 and 28; Apr. 9,
16, and 26; June 4; July 7, 8, 16, and 28; Aug. 16; Sept. 13; Oct.
25 and 26; Nov. 13 and 17; Dec. 20, 21, 24, 27, 29, and 31.

Schimmel, Annemarie. *My Soul Is a Woman: the Feminine in
Islam.* New York: Continuum, 1997: Jan. 6 and 8; Apr. 2.

Schuon, Frijthof. *Understanding Islam.* New York: Roy
Publishers, 1963: Apr. 20; Nov. 17. REPRINTED BY PERMISSION OF
WORLD WISDOM.

Shabistari, Mahmud. *The Secret Rose Garden.* Edited by D. R.
Fideler. Grand Rapid, MI: 2002: Jan. 18; Apr. 15.

Skali, Faouzi. *Traces de lumière, Paroles initiatiques soufies.* Paris:
Éditions Albin Michel, 1996: Jan. 1, 7, 9, 14, 16, 23, and 25; Feb.
10, 20, 26, and 27; Mar. 2, 8, 9, 13, 14, 17, and 26; Apr. 30; May
5, 7, 8, 15, 17, 25, and 31; June 20, 22, 23, 24, and 26; July 2, 3,
13, 23, 24, 25, 27, and 31; Aug. 6, 9, and 22; Sept. 2; Oct. 1, 18,
21, and 22; Nov. 1, 9, and 30; Dec. 4, 7, 17, 21, 26, and 30.

The Talmud: Nov. 13.

al-Tawhidi, Abu Hayyan. *De l'Amitié.* Arles,
France: Éditions Actes Sud, 2006: Apr. 11; May 29;
Sept. 21; Nov. 20.

Saint Thomas. *L'Évangile de Thomas.* Translated and edited by
Jean-Yves Leloup. Paris: Éditions Albin Michel, 1986: July 18.

Varenne, Jean. *Zarathushtra et la tradition mazdéenne.* Paris:
Éditions du Seuil, 2006.

Vitray-Meyerovitch, Eva de. *Rumi and Sufism.* Sausalito, CA:
Post-Apollo Press, 1987: Jan. 15, 28, and 30; Feb. 8; Oct. 10 and
20; Dec. 5, 9, 11, and 15.

Yunus, Muhammad. "Transgresser les préjugés économiques," *Le
Monde diplomatique,* December 1997: Nov. 28.

Acknowledgments

To André & Jaffa Stockhammer for their unwavering support and unfailing friendship

The authors extend their warmest thanks to those who helped, advised, and supported them
in the making of *Devotions: Wisdom from the Cradle of Civilization*

Global study

Universita Cattolica del Sacro Cuore: Professor Paolo Branca and his assistant Joan Rundo in Milan (Italy)

The University of Leyden in the Netherlands

Rimay-Nalanda University and Sangha Rimay International in Arvillard (France)

The Ribat Al Fath Association for sustainable development in Rabat (Morocco)

Osmund Bopearachchi, Accredited Professor at the Université de Paris, la Sorbonne, CNRS archeology lab (France)

Father Carney Gavin, President, Archives for Historical Documentation in Brighton (Great Britain)

Father Maximus El-Anthony of the Monastery of Saint Anthony (Egypt)

Father Jean-Jacques Perennes, head of the Spiritual Library in Cairo (Egypt)

Yetta and John Goelet in Sandricourt (France)

Hossein T. Akrad in Amsterdam (Netherlands)

Pierre and Josée Godé in Paris (France)

Évelyne and Costa Vrousos in Saint-Ismier and Calina Lauer in Strasbourg (France)

Jaffa & André Stockhammer in Geneva (Switzerland)

Guy & Nathalie Trouveroy, former Belgian Ambassador in Cairo (Egypt)

Alain Guillemin, at the Institute of the Arab World in Paris (France)

Literary advisers

Françoise Toussaint in Paris, Pascale Manificat in Briançon, Jean-François Cludy, Michel Bessis, Ionna Rapti, Céline Anger in Paris (France), Jean Daniel Hostettler and Martine Jaccard in Lausanne (Switzerland)

Literary research assistance

Virginie de Borchgrave d'Altena in Brussels (Belgium)

Emmanuelle Courson in Annecy (France)

Logistical and administrative support
Madeleine Viviani and Annalisa Beltrami at the Swiss
Commission for UNESCO in Bern (Switzerland)
Franck Portelance and Edith Coiquaud of FUJIFILM in Paris
(France)
Guy Frangeul and Bertrand Nauts of Objectif Bastille in Paris
(France)
Bernard Gachet, Philippe Lavorel, and Jean Baptiste Deprez in
Annecy (France)
Pascal Maubert, French Consul in Beijing (China)
Jean-Luc Delvert, French Consul in Bangkok (Thailand)
Gabriela Perez Palma in Brussels (Belgium)

Travel preparation
Virginie de Borchgrave d'Altena in Brussels (Belgium)

Photographic assistance in the field
Noonie Varunee Skaosang (Thailand)
Jacky Wen Yutao (China)

Photo selection
Guy de Régibus in Paris (France)

Algeria
Muhammad Bekakra and his family in El Oued, as well as Fariza,
Soumaya, Nadia, Khatir

Egypt
Dominique Escartin and Noha Escartin in Paris; Fatima Ebayd
Muhammad, Habibah Ebayd Muhammad, Azizah Beshir Jumah,
Esraa and Safaa Gamal in Gharb es-Sehel, Saiid Muhammad
Hudsan in Assouan, Victor Garo in Luxor, Father Thomas and
Father Abader at the Monastery of Saint Paul, Father Nicodemos
and Father Daood at the Monastery of Saint Bishoy in Egypt

Iran
Maryam, Sarvenaz, Nashreen, Ali in Isfahan, Mehdi and Mah in
Tehran; Frédéric Garouste in Paris; Saeed Sadraee in Brussels

Israel and Palestine
Emmanuel Abramowicz, Céline Moulys, Father Marie Angel of
the Saint John Community, Jean Emmanuel Lagarde and Alain
Borne in Paris, Alexandra Tissinié in Nice, France; Ameer Basti,
Dr Catharina Wolff at the Austrian Hospice of the
Holy Family, Jeffrey Seidel, Jodie and Eden in
Jerusalem

Jordan
Dr Ahmad Masa'deh,
Ambassador of the
Hashemite Kingdom
of Jordan in Brussels;
Mona al Husseini,

Communications Director at the Embassy of the Hashemite Kingdom of Jordan in Paris; Taman and Nasser in Petra, Jordan

Lebanon
Alma Fakhre Mecattaf, Thilda Herbillon-Moubayed, Abdallah Naaman, Cultural Attaché at the Lebanese Embassy in Paris; Maggy Chamoun, Zaina Trad in Brussels

Libya
Beshir Trabelsi of the Sand & Ruins Tours agency, along with Abdul Aziz Chembira and Muhammad Abubak, Otman Abul Aziz, Muhammad Tergui in Sebha, Vittorio and Luisa Rocco di Torrepadula, minister at the Italian Embassy in Tripoli

Morocco
Claudie and Khalid Benchegra, Khalid Afalou in Marrakech; Quentin Wilbaux in Brussels

Mongolia, Kyrgyzstan, Turkmenistan, and the Sinkiang province of China
René Collet in Courchevel, Marie-Eudes Lauriot Prevost in Paris; Naraa Tenger-Ekh and Muugii Munkhjargal in Ulan Bator, Mongolia; Pierre Jaccard and Philippe Chabloz in Geneva, Switzerland; Dalbaev Kanatbek in Bishkek, Kyrgyzstan

The Sultanate of Oman
Bakheit bin Abdulla bin Salim Bait Masam in Oman

Pakistan
Zishan Afzal Khan in Islamabad, Pakistan

Turkey
Fesih Sevdi, Ahmet Ertug, Ara Güler, Lütfi Aygüler and family, Ismet and Mahmut Bozbey in Istanbul

Yemen
Mrs. Khadija al-Salami at the Embassy of Yemen in Paris; Mr. Gilles Gauthier, French Ambassador in Sanaa; Corinne Tarhouni, Nadil and Muhammad Al-Nuzaili of the BTA Tours agency in Sanaa; Osama Taher and Adel Ali, Abdulsalam A. Senter, Muhammad A. al-Yereemi, Ahmed Abdo Hamzah, Muhammad H. al-Ansey, and the family of Abdullah M. al-Agel in Manakha, Yemen

The following provided the energy necessary to make _Devotions_ happen:

At the Föllmi Workshops in Annecy, France
Viviane Bizien, Emmanuelle Courson, Christelle Chaffard, Marion Franck, Stéphanie Ly, Corinne Morvan-Sedik, Sophie Pouly, and Nicolas Pasquier

At Éditions de La Martinière in Paris
Isabelle Perrod, Sandrine Bailly, Dominique Escartin, Cécile Vandenbroucque, Marianne Lassandro, and their teams

Special thanks to Hervé de La Martinière for his loyal support and deep trust.

Photograph (October 7) © Noonie Varunee Skaosang

By the same authors, in the Offerings for Humanity series:

Awakenings: Asian Wisdom for every Day
Revelations: Latin American Wisdom for Every Day
(also available in Spanish)
Origins: African Wisdom for Every Day
Wisdom: 365 Thoughts from Indian Masters
Offerings: Buddhist Wisdom for Every Day

At the same publisher,
by Olivier Föllmi:

Asia
Latin America
Africa
India
Homage to the Himalayas

www.follmi.com

Devotions: Wisdom from the Cradle of Civilization is the sixth volume in the Offerings for Humanity series promoting the spiritual heritage of mankind.

This seven-year project, begun in 2003, was initiated thanks to the generosity of an anonymous donor and of Lotus & Yves Mahé.

The project is actively supported by Fujifilm, Canon, and Sangha Rimay International.

With the participation of Dupon, Orkis, and Grands Reportages.
The Offerings for Humanity project enjoys the active patronage of UNESCO.

FUJIFILM **Canon**

Selected text translated from the French by Nicholas Elliott

English-Language Edition:
Magali Veillon, Project Manager
Sheila Friedling, Editor
Shawn Dahl, Designer
Michelle Ishay and Neil Egan, Jacket design
Jules Thomson, Production Manager

Library of Congress Cataloging-in-Publication Data
Föllmi, Danielle.
    Devotions : wisdom from the cradle of civilization / by Danielle and Olivier Föllmi.
        p. cm.
    Includes bibliographical references and index.
    ISBN 978-0-8109-7113-4
        1. Spiritual life—Quotations, maxims, etc. 2. Middle East—Pictorial works.
    I. Föllmi, Olivier, 1958– II. Title.

    BL624.F635 2008
    204'32—dc22
                    2008025578

Copyright © 2008 Éditions de La Martinière, an imprint of
La Martinière Groupe, Paris/Éditions Föllmi, Annecy, France
English translation copyright © 2008 Abrams, New York

Printed and bound in China
10 9 8 7 6 5 4 3 2 1

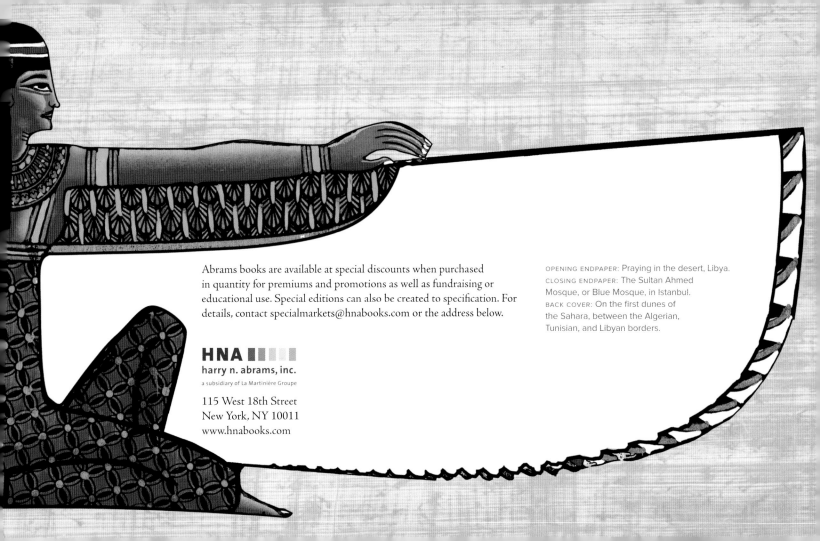

Abrams books are available at special discounts when purchased in quantity for premiums and promotions as well as fundraising or educational use. Special editions can also be created to specification. For details, contact specialmarkets@hnabooks.com or the address below.

HNA ▊▊▊▊▊
harry n. abrams, inc.
a subsidiary of La Martinière Groupe

115 West 18th Street
New York, NY 10011
www.hnabooks.com

OPENING ENDPAPER: Praying in the desert, Libya.
CLOSING ENDPAPER: The Sultan Ahmed Mosque, or Blue Mosque, in Istanbul.
BACK COVER: On the first dunes of the Sahara, between the Algerian, Tunisian, and Libyan borders.

Shalom aleichem. As-salāmu ʿalaykum.

Peace be upon you.

Men and women wish for one another the peace that begins in the heart of each person. A gesture accompanies this expression by which the hand is lifted from heart to mouth and from mouth to forehead before tracing the pattern of an arabesque that sums up the three mysteries: the body, speech, and thought.

At the very moment that we speak, stars are born and others disappear.

How glorious!

Khaled Bentounès
20TH–21ST CENTURY